Praise for The Elliptical Dialogue

"At a time when much of the world is preoccupied with its borders and the tensions between preserving safety and identity versus an open freedom of movement across borders, Midbøe's book is an original and refreshing contribution to the creativity and value that can emerge from occupying comfortably a borderland position. Midbøe brings her experience as a Jungian analyst in clinical practice and a fine intellect to bear to develop what she calls an elliptical dialogue, a map to orientate the reader to a contemporary and useable model of the analytic relationship in clinical work. Jung emphasized strongly the role of the relationship between the patient and the analyst and the potential for this relationship to bring opportunities for growth and healing. Midbøe combines three different fields of study, systems theory, the theory of linguistics and Jungian psychology as a framework for understanding the connections between the intrapsychic and the interpersonal worlds of the individual. The book is well-written, accessible with theory and practice woven beautifully together so that the role the analyst and his/her psychic processes play within the elliptical dialogue may be clearly observed. The book makes a first-rate contribution to both theory and practice, and should be on the reading list of every training institute."

-Jan Wiener, Director of Training, Society of Analytical Psychology, London; Vice President, IAAP, 2010 to 2013

Gunilla Midbøe

The Elliptical Dialogue

A Communications Model for Psychotherapy

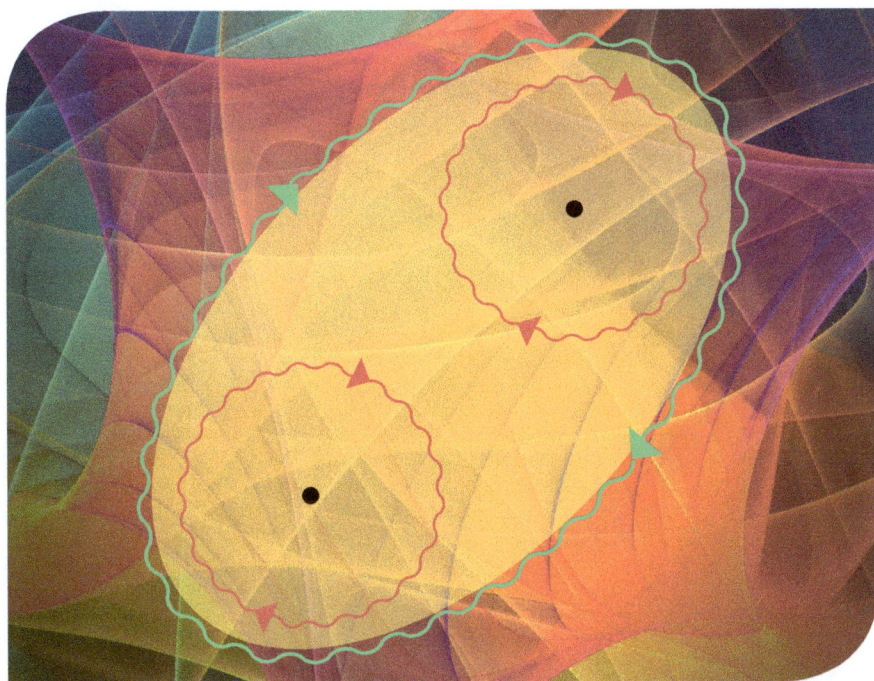

CHIRON
PUBLICATIONS

Chiron Publications
Asheville, North Carolina

ChironPublicatons.com

Interior and cover design by Lisa Alford
Printed primarily in the United States of America

ISBN 978-1-63051-417-4 paperback
ISBN 978-1-63051-418-1 hardcover
ISBN 978-1-63051-419-8 electronic

Library of Congress Cataloging-in-Publication
Names: Midbøe, Gunilla, author.
Title: The elliptical dialogue : a communications model for psychotherapy / Gunilla Midbøe.
Description: Asheville, North Carolina : Chiron Publications, [2017] | Includes bibliographical references and index.
Identifiers: LCCN 2017004634 (print) | LCCN 2017016973 (ebook) | ISBN 9781630514198 (E-book) | ISBN 9781630514174 (pbk. : alk. paper) | ISBN 9781630514181 (hardcover : alk. paper)
Subjects: LCSH: Jungian psychology. | Psychoanalysis. | Psychotherapy.
Classification: LCC BF173.J85 (ebook) | LCC BF173.J85 M53 2017 (print) | DDC 150.19/54--dc23
LC record available at https://lccn.loc.gov/2017004634

Tomas Tranströmer New Collected Poems, tran. Robin Fulton (Bloodaxe Books, 2011)
Reproduced with permission of Bloodaxe Books.
bloodaxebooks.com

DEDICATION

To my family, past, present and thriving, who helped me

experience the relational essence of elliptical dialogue

in my mind and body.

FOREWORD
Murray Stein

I am pleased to introduce Gunilla Midbøe's work to an international audience. I do this with the hope and confidence that it will find resonance with a wide and diverse audience of psychotherapists and counselors. In fact, for anyone who works with others in an advisory or counseling role, including consultants to individuals in the organizational and business worlds, such as executive coaches, this work offers many helpful ideas about what can transpire in consistent interpersonal interactions that extend over a period of time. I should also include within this potential audience parents and teachers. Midbøe's perspectives, as laid out in this book before you, will take you deeper into an appreciation of the complexity and the beauty of all relationships that matter.

What is a dialogue in depth? And how do you know that you have engaged on one? Dialogue is a precious human capacity to exchange thoughts, feelings, perceptions and all subjective contents, even dreams and fantasies, with another person and get a response. Psychotherapy as it is generally practiced today, no matter what theoretical school one might be trained in, relies on the healing power of dialogue. Dialogue is more than a simple back-and-forth exchange of opinions. It generates an alchemy, and it is this alchemical process that has the power to change people in their subjectivity. This means, not only in their opinions and conscious views, i.e., cognitively, but in their emotions and even deeper in their ways of processing experience through their complex psychological make-up, their unconscious parts. Dialogue touches the depths of the soul and makes a difference. You know that you've engaged in a true dialogue when you realize that something has been profoundly changed in your way of being. It is a kind of conversion experience.

As Midbøe discusses the transformative interaction between therapist and client by elaborating on what she calls "the elliptical dialogue," one gets a vivid impression of how this process comes into being and actually works in longterm psychotherapy. The value of her descriptions lies in the clear articulation of dimensions and boundaries. This is a contained dialogue in depth, and so there are both horizontal and vertical dimensionalities. Each partner in the dialogue assists in containing the process within the professional relationship but also in exposing the depth of the psyche and bringing it into the process. In the psychoanalytic tradition, this has been spoken of as transference-and-countertransference dynamics. What gives Midbøe's account the edge over others is the image she brings to the discussion. It is ingenious and most helpful in sorting out the facets of the dialogic interactions. In the elliptical field one senses the movement of energy in several dimensions, and also its containment. It is this combination of dynamics and containment that gives the elliptical dialogue its power to transform.

A particularly Jungian feature of Midbøe's account of the therapeutic process is that it places the therapist squarely into the midst of the encounter. The elliptical image contains two centers, each engaged with the other in an energized field. The therapist does not stand outside of the process. The implication of this is that both partners in the dialogue are subject to the process and to the transformative effects it produces. Both therapist and client are changed by the encounter.

The discussion here is not only based on theory, Jungian and other, but deeply grounded in practical experience. Case material illustrates the use and value of the elliptical dialogue, as well as the results. Because Midbøe is such a seasoned clinician, her case descriptions are complex and thick with detail. It is the combination of image and word that makes for a construction both vivid and convincing. One cautionary note would be that not all of her readers will have the depth of experience she has and may find some of the discussion daunting. Her cases are not beginner's cases and they show the hand of a skilled and well trained clinician.

Because the elliptical dialogue takes form in language, I find it exceptionally valuable that Midbøe draws on the genius of the philosopher, Ludwig Wittgenstein, for insight into the importance of language in the dialogue. Midbøe shows that often the simplest word occurring in a throw away sentence uttered by the client can hold the key to opening the dialogue to the deepest sort of reflection and insight. Sensitivity to nuances in language used is essential to fostering the development of the dialogue and lending it transformative impact. Midbøe attends words like the alchemist attends her furnaces and vessels. One could build on what Maria Prophetessa, the ancient alchemist, said of the vessel, "the vas is all," by saying that for the elliptical dialogue "the word is the vas" and as such is everything. I applaud Midbøe for bringing Wittgenstein into the discussion. This may be a first among analytical psychologists.

As well, I applaud her for bringing Gregory Bateson into play in this presentation of the therapeutic process. It is Midbøe's previous training in systems theory and Bateson's work in bringing this into behavior science that sensitizes her to the familial and cultural contexts that come into the elliptical dialogue. In fact, the elliptical dialogue is a kind of "system" at play between two people within the containment of the therapeutic relationship.

What I like most about this book is the lively impression it gives of what happens in the psychotherapeutic relationship. Things are constantly in motion; there is give and take; there are many dimensions simultaneously in play. And all of this is contained within the framework of professional and ethical responsibility, a temenos or sacred space that exists today within our secular world. It is a space where people can come to themselves in caring interaction with another. Midbøe shows us clear examples of how this comes about in her practice, and she shows us how we may also bring such lively movement of the psyche into play in our practices.

Murray Stein

Murray Stein, Ph.D. is a Jungian psychoanalyst practicing in Zurich, Switzerland and a training and supervising analyst at the International School of Analytical Psychology in Zurich (ISAPZurich). He is the author of numerous books, including *Jung's Map of the Soul* and *Minding the Self*.

PREFACE

I have always had a relationship with border crossings. As a child living on the border between Sweden and Norway, I was often told to be a "margarine kid," which meant sitting with a number of friends in the back seat of the car so that the driver could justify the transport of a larger amount of sugar, margarine and flour as we passed the tollbooth. The more passengers we had in the car, the more groceries we were allowed to import without paying customs duty. I remember cheering every time we crossed the border successfully!

The border is also a very distinct part of the landscape because a Peace Monument was erected here in 1914. This 18-meter-tall granite monument can be seen from both the road and the railway, and was erected to celebrate 100 years of peace between Sweden and Norway. In my youth a popular radio show called *Morokulien* – Across All Borders transmitted from this monument, hosted by Swedish and Norwegian radio. The name *Morokulien* (the Norwegian word *moro* and the Swedish word *kul* mean "joy") then became the name of the designated territory between the countries. You can actually become a citizen of Morokulien and have a passport! In 2014, Norway and Sweden celebrated 200 years of peace. For people coming from countries in which the borders are closed and marked by hostility, Morokulien can be a very powerful experience. For example, when a South Korean couple crossed the border from Sweden, they were moved to tears when the Norwegian tourist officer welcomed them to Norway and shook them by the hand. For them, walking across the border and continuing their journey was a moving and personal experience. In their country, the border between North and South Korea is closed. In contrast, the border between Sweden and Norway is marked by a peace monument, and in people's minds the border symbolizes trade and an exchange of mutually creative projects.

Later in life I became the first member of our family to go to university, which meant that I moved away from my family and their working-class identity and values. Although they continued to encourage me, when I returned home for the holidays, they did not really recognize me, and I found it difficult to articulate my experiences in a way they could understand. A meeting of hearts and minds became increasingly difficult. I had become an alien and too strange to comprehend. In a sense, a class journey never ends and has no final destination. It also involves the crossing of borders.

These border crossings triggered the question of dialoguing in depth with strangers. I asked myself what a depth dialogue was. Was it an internal dialogue between my conscious self and an inner "other," or a dialogue between me and another person?

As a symbol for both types of dialogue, which seem to me to be asymmetrical yet harmonious, I turn to the Greek god Hermes to guide my thinking about communication, movement, and journeying. Depth dialogue is both a movement and a journey. Hermes is equally at home in the depths of the unconscious world and on the heights of the spiritual world, and is able to link them to each other and to the middle world of ordinary human consciousness. Hermes, in his winged sandals, is always on the move. If you encounter him in images, in your imagination or in action in your inner or outer life, he will bring great gifts as well as play tricks on you. In my inner world as a young woman, I met the mercurial element of Hermes in my reading, where different worlds and perspectives were made visible through the words, images and stories. Studies and reading sparked off and energized my own journey. Without me being aware of it, Hermes introduced me to analytical psychology. Somehow, Erich Neumann's *Amor and Psyche: The Psychic Development of the Feminine*, a Commentary on the Tale by Apuleius, fell into my hands. What a gift! A gift for life.

Cultural and personal experiences like this are part of my professional journey, which is why in this book I have ventured to cross borders and gather perspectives from three quite different fields of study: systems and communications theory (Gregory Bateson), linguistic theory (Ludwig Wittgenstein), and psychological theory (C. G. Jung). I have woven them together with hermeneutics. Hermeneutics is understood as a circular and spiral movement where one's own tradition and horizon of understanding is in dialogue with those of others in the past, present, and an imagined future.

This was my inner process as my life's journey unfolded and is also how the image of an elliptical dialogue came into being. I was and have remained an individual in the borderland. I like it there and am comfortable.

I initially trained as a social worker. During the 1970s, when I started my professional career, values like international solidarity, gender equality, and a socialistic political system were shared by almost every social worker. For me, this was a way of developing the working-class values that I had grown up with into a more conscious and reflected stance in my later life and work. In addition, international influences from psychodynamic theory and practice began to permeate the social and psychiatric health care systems in Sweden. Professionals like Murray Jackson, Virginia Satir, and other leading psychotherapists came to Sweden, held workshops, and offered supervision. We watched the English film *Family Life*, which had been influenced by the theories of Ronald Laing. One day I went to a book sale and found *Människan och hennes Symboler (Man and His Symbols)* by C.G. Jung and other Jungian authors. I was deeply impressed by the text. It also equipped me with a language for describing the unconscious levels of reality in myself and in the collective. It also made it possible to understand the dynamics in society from a depth perspective.

I have worked in the mental health care system in Sweden for many years now. Working with families and couples in the fields of child psychiatry and family counseling, I now include family systems theory in my methods of treatment. Its founder was Gregory Bateson, and his ideas have helped me to create a kind of dialogue among family members that helps them to change their behaviour – and also my own behaviour as a psychotherapist. I also adopted the language theory of Wittgenstein in order to create deeper levels of communication. However, at a certain point I reached a limit and felt that both my professional perspectives and my personal life had to change and go deeper. I felt a strong need to work with individuals and to develop deeper dialogues.

What I have experienced in my own family, both in the present and the past (such as losing my father when I was 13) has made it easier for me go deeper into my own self-knowledge and to see how this has affected and affects my life. I remember once having a powerful, frightening, and raw dream that a wolverine was clutching my right foot and I could not shake her off. This dream prompted me to go into analysis, and I was fortunate to have Stina Thyberg as my personal analyst. Stina was the first Jungian psychoanalyst in Sweden. She had returned to Sweden at the beginning of 1970s after studying at the Jung Institute in Zürich. With Stina's help, the dream symbol of the wolverine also became a source of creativity, in that with the aid of amplification and active imagination, it helped to develop my conscious mind. After a while, the wolverine turned into a little girl who was hard to please. Stina suggested that I put her on my lap and talk to her, but also listen to her story. So we—the little girl within and my conscious I—began a dialogue. I have to admit that

I was not very enamoured with this project at first, because I did not want to identify with the cranky and sour little girl, who was both demanding and angry. But this was part of what Stina called my shadow work; hard to take on board and make conscious, but a side of myself that required consciousness and integration. In my active imagination dialogue, the little girl told me that she was sad and was mourning the losses in her life. In the end I was able to listen to her and have a dialogue. With Stina's support, I was able to get rid of several complexes and continue my individuation process.

It is important here to underline Jung's view of the human psyche. At both the conscious and unconscious levels, it is potentially creative for us to meet, greet, and enter into a dialogic imagination with our shadow selves and to keep the different polarities of our psyche apart, without acting them out in destructive behaviour.

At this crucial point in my work, at the beginning of 1990, I also discovered a direct relationship between Gregory Bateson and Jung. This was important, because it made me think about the inner relationship between the three thinkers who had been so important to me in my professional journey. What unites the theoretical perspectives of Bateson, Wittgenstein, and Jung is the recognition of a spiritual dimension – via nature in Bateson's case, via language for Wittgenstein, and via depth psychology and alchemy for Jung.

In my own case, I realized that I had to let go of my defences and enter a state of liminality, where the border becomes a space in its own right. I think of liminality as a domain with one line – one end of the line leading down toward the deep archetypal layers of the collective and personal unconscious, and the other end of the line leading upward and forward toward spiritual energies that are beyond our conscious awareness. In the middle of the line, there is a small "I," trying to make sense of a personal individuation journey. For me, this journey has woven together my personal and my professional life. Some of this story will be made visible in this book.

ACKNOWLEDGEMENTS

Many experiences of elliptical dialogues have contributed to the writings of this book. In my professional individuation journey first and foremost the deep, rich and changing encounters with all of you in my analytical practice, supervision settings and in lecturing. I am deeply grateful for our mutual experience.

For my own Jungian analysts, supervisors and colleagues in the Nordic countries, in Switzerland and in other parts of the world - you all know who you are and you will always be there in my inner world. Together we experienced dialogues and tensions journeying into wild, dark and unmapped land but always with the aim of exploring meaning and trying to find the spark of creativity. With attentive compassion you helped me gain consciousness of the inner and outer importance of relationships and dialogues. You also made me see that writing could be included in my individuation journey.

A warm heartfelt thanks also goes to Chiron Publications for providing a final holding container for my script and giving it the form of this book. The firm, clear and supportive editing made me go into the final process of writing with deeply felt confidence and trust.

And a generous grant from the Swedish C G Jung Foundation came in the right moment of completion of fulfilling the manuscript into a book. Much appreciated!

And finally, for Lars, always being there with love and support.

Introduction

Jungian psychoanalysis is firmly grounded in relational dynamics, that is, in the mutuality of the partners in the psychoanalytical setting and the full recognition of each person's autonomy. This relational setup is also what human beings struggle with in their communities, families, and professional relationships. Communication is thus the cornerstone of Jungian psychoanalysis.

This book focuses on communication from the perspective of the implicit and explicit dialogue that emerges in Jungian psychoanalysis. This dialogue is a meeting of minds in a specially designed and created psychotherapeutic space. The book is also written from the perspective of a dialogue that has developed from the three theories referred to in the preface. My hope is that the book will be of use to colleagues in the profession and to anyone who is interested in analytical psychology and curious about Jungian psychoanalysis.

I think of what follows as a journey and the reader as someone traveling with me on that journey. In this sense, I regard myself as both a guide and a companion. A journey can take different forms, such as the journey through life and the everyday travel of the commuter. What is common to all journeys is that they never really follow the map that is etched out in the inner world of the imagination. This is another way of saying that "the map is not the territory," as the Russian-American independent scholar Alfred Korzybski (1879-1950) so eloquently put it. While it is good to make plans and draw maps, it is also important to keep in mind that the territory is not the map, although we might hope that something in our inner images will align with our experience and that the difference between reality and image will not be too great. We might be able to imagine relational dynamics as a dialogue that will help us to develop, both in our lives and in the professional work of psychotherapy. This is, at least, the goal of this present work.

I remember when I first became aware of Jung as a possible companion on my personal and professional journey. I had an inkling that he was lurking somewhere in the shadows. While reading an article in *Family Therapy Networker* (Luepnitz, D. 1988), I discovered a connection between Jung and Gregory Bateson, one of the founders of systems theory. From that moment on, Jung and analytical psychology came more fully into view. Since then, I have studied Jung's writings and the works of others in the school of analytical psychology. These studies, together with the subsequent training I received to become a Jungian psychoanalyst, have enabled me to growth and to understand my inner and outer reality.

Jung became an assistant at Burghölzli Mental Hospital in Zürich on November 10, 1900, when he was 26. He was glad to move away from Basel, where his mother and sister lived and where he was mainly identified as the son of Reverend Paul Jung and the grandson of Professor Carl Gustav Jung. In Zürich, he was free to relate to the world from his own horizon. In the years that followed, as a practising psychiatrist, he laid the foundations for analytical psychology and his own individuation journey.

At Burghölzli, Jung worked under the leadership of Professor Eugene Bleuler. The culture of the mental hospital was very special. Many of the nurses, doctors, and other employees lived in the hospital grounds, where they cultivated vegetables and fruit and raised animals, which also provided work for the patients. As a small village with closed borders, it became a target for all kinds of projections. In this special culture, Jung met psychotic individuals and was responsible for their treatment. He approached them with a mixture of curiosity and humanity. He wrote in his autobiography, *Memories, Dreams, Reflections*: "In many cases in psychiatry, the patient who comes to us has a story that is not told, and which as a rule no one knows of. To my mind therapy only really begins after the investigation of that wholly personal story" (Jung 1961/1989).

Babette S. had been diagnosed with psychosis when Jung met her at the Burghölzli Klinik. It is interesting to read Jung's reflections on her personal history and how he entered into a dialogue with her. Babette helped him to understand the language of schizophrenics, an experience that led him to formulate what he regarded as the basic humanist values of the therapist in the interpersonal relationship: "The crucial point is that I confront the patient as one human being to another. Analysis is a dialogue demanding two partners.

Analyst and patient sit facing one another, eye to eye; the doctor has something to say, but so has the patient" (Jung 1961/1989).

At the beginning of his psychiatric career, Jung worked extensively with the Word Association Experiment (WAE) and published *Studies in Word Association* (1903). In 1907, he met Freud and, in the years that followed, collaborated with him to create the International Psychoanalytic Association (IPA), of which he became the first president. In 1912, he broke with Freud and his psychoanalysis and formed his own movement called analytical psychology. While still at Burghölzli, he wrote a groundbreaking manuscript on dementia praecox (schizophrenia) and was the first psychiatrist to introduce the hypothesis of its psychogenesis (National Encyclopaedia, 1993, p. 252, issue 10. Jung 1907/1981.)

Jung's work with WAE and his famous theory of complexes are still relevant today in terms of how we understand our patients and their families. WAE indicates how words can be highly charged with affect for a person in dialogue with others, to the extent that certain words can produce reactions that are both visible to the onlooker and felt within the body. Such reactions, identified by so-called complex indicators, have roots in a person's history and are often connected to the family at the unconscious level. These reactions may be experienced as painful and filled with conflict and need to be worked through in analysis or family psychotherapy.

This is why attentiveness to the language used and the reactions to this in the analytical dialogue is so important. Both the language and the reactions can serve as openers and guides to a deeper understanding and mapping of the unconscious. Based on his discoveries using WAE, Jung went on to develop the theory of complexes as unconscious content filled with affect and having an archetypal core. Everyone has complexes. They are energetic and indicate a need for greater consciousness when they become visible as bodily reactions, verbal outbursts, dreams, thoughts, and fantasies. Contemporary affect theory, as formulated by Silvan Tomkins (Tomkins, 1962, 1963) and developed further by Edward Tronick (2007), can be seen to stem from Jung's theory of complexes. When tracking the various appearances of a complex in analytical work, I have come to see how what I call the elliptical dialogue could contribute to an understanding of how a complex phenomenon can emerge from an unconscious core and move toward consciousness.

In the first part of this book I introduce the idea of the elliptical dialogue as a way of understanding and connecting intrapsychic and interpersonal relationships. This emerged as a structure when I saw the connection between systems theory, analytical psychology and language. In my clinical experience with individuals, couples and families, and in my experience of supervision and education, the elliptical dialogue has proved to be a useful image for linking these fields in a practical and theoretical way.

In the collective consciousness of our global world, it is interesting to reflect on how humans have always felt the need to orient themselves using maps. Here I am not just talking about cartographic maps, but maps for making the gap between our conscious and unconscious selves more bearable. Physiologically researchers have recently succeeded in locating the "GPS gene" in rats and can thus show that the need to map is built into our biological system. The Nobel Prize in Physiology or Medicine 2014 was shared and one half went to May-Britt and Edvard I. Moser for their discoveries of cells that constitute a positioning system in the brain.

In *Abysmal* (2007), the geographer Gunnar Olsson offers a perspective from culture, philosophy, and Western thinking about how we create maps in our rational mind. However, many psychological maps also take account of the irrational, unknown, and unconscious energy of the collective and the individual universe and cosmos. C.G. Jung discovered this early on in life when the text for *Septem Sermones ad Mortuos* (The Seven Sermons to the Dead) came to him and had to be written down (1916). He also constructed his cosmographic map, or mandala, *Systema Munditotius* (The system of all worlds) in the same year. Both the text and the map have a transformative energy, so that when reading the words and entering the map, the transcendent power that connects consciousness with the unknown in a dialogue can easily be sensed. Similarly, the elliptical dialogue model and other psychotherapeutic maps also open the doors to the unconscious human psyche.

An important instigating spark for the elliptical dialogue model was the analytical work that "Björn" and I were engaged in. The case of "Björn" (the name means bear in Swedish) is representative of many of my analysands and is a fractal of a kaleidoscopic clinical experience. In Swedish, the word björn (bear) can be the symbolic carrier of polarity between teddy bear and predator. In the book it is used as an integrated symbol for the flows, difficulties, ruptures, and mutual experiences that are encountered in a Jungian analytical individuation process. The focus here is on the hermeneutics of the liminal space between partners in an inner and outer dialogue. The elliptical dialogue models both the micro- and macro-processes that take place within the analytical space and in the exchanges between the participants. For both the therapist and the patient, an important question is: What happens in our minds and what do we put into words? This is where my curiosity takes me when reflecting on the relational dynamics of Jungian psychoanalysis and psychotherapy. A description of the elliptical dialogue and its relevance for transformative relationships forms the first part of this book.

Hermeneutics, based on dialogue as formulated by Hans-Georg Gadamer (2003), is a contemporary starting point for understanding the elliptical dialogue as a map or model for communication in psychotherapy. Gadamer insists on dialogical-based hermeneutics because, according to him, this is where the dialogue becomes active and engages both participants. It is here, in a space that allows for a common language, that the other person's reality can be understood. Together with Gregory Bateson's family systems theory and Carl Gustav Jung's analytical psychology, Ludwig Wittgenstein's philosophy of language, what he calls the language game, forms the "base camp" of the elliptical dialogue. Wittgenstein's theory was first outlined in his *Tractatus logico-philosophicus* (1961/1992) as the picture theory of language and was later developed in *Philosophical Investigations* (1953/1992) as the language game. The analogy between language and game demonstrates that the meanings of words depend on how they are used in the various and diverse contexts of human life. The concept is not meant to suggest that there is anything trivial about language or that language is "just a game." On the contrary, from the very beginning, psychoanalysis was regarded as a dialogue and as a therapeutic encounter between two people who used language to understand unconscious attitudes and complexes. When looking at the use and expression of language within the context of psychotherapy or supervision, I think that both Wittgenstein and the French philosopher Gaston Bachelard (1884-1963) show that we are relational, poetical, and dialogical individuals. Bachelard (1958/1994, 1960/1971) refers to both C.G. Jung and E. Neumann in his work on the power of poetic language and the experience of intimate places, where we can reconnect in new and unique ways of expanding consciousness within language. Thus, dialogically structured language is important in the liminal space of the elliptical dialogue. Here I would like to draw attention to our use of language as psychoanalysts and psychotherapists. This is crucial, especially with regard to how we formulate questions to ourselves and within ourselves. In this liminal space we find language in the shape of the spoken word and body language and in the transference relationships between myself and the other. Here I think that Jung's works *The Transcendent Function* (1916/1981) and *The Psychology of the Transference* (1946/1981) help to create ways of being and bring new responses to our words and actions into the liminal space of the elliptical dialogue.

In the second part of the book, I describe the clinical applications of the model and consider how transformation in Jungian psychoanalysis can be understood. Using three clinical vignettes, I demonstrate how the model can widen our perspectives of understanding. These clinical narratives demonstrate how work within the elliptical dialogue in the psychotherapeutic practice can be carried out.

Concepts like transference and projection are well-known in the context of depth psychological theory. The elliptical dialogue model puts verbal exchange into a depth psychology perspective, not only as words spoken but also as a language that is charged with symbols, many of which are often just below the surface of conscious awareness. The psychotherapist is responsible for using words in a way that promotes change and movement, while at the same time realising that the words spoken in the context of the relationship can help to deepen understanding and a sense of self. The spotlight is on the liminal spaces contained within language. If we are only exposed to the language games we know and are familiar with, we are likely to stay the same. If we encounter something unusual in a dialogue, it could induce change. However, if that new language is too unfamiliar and unusual, we tend to back off, close up, and retreat to our comfort zones. This is what happened to me when I returned home to my family after my university studies. Our language contexts had become too unusual, and our elliptical dialogue broke down. As psychotherapists, we try to create a safe space that allows for the unusual but that does not block the ongoing elliptical dialogue. It is my intention to explore this liminal space of inner and outer dialogues in our Jungian psychoanalytical work.

The notion of the transcendent function is important in Jungian psychoanalytical work and refers to the synthesised view of the psychic process in analytical treatment. This synthesising process of opposites develops in interpersonal relationships and in the intrapsychic processes of the analyst and analysand. Jung wrote about this relational dynamic in an essay in 1916, which remained undiscovered in his files until 1953. In *The Transcendent Function* (Jung 1953/1981), Jung describes the concept of *active imagination* as an auxiliary way of developing deeper contact with the unconscious layers that lie beneath the threshold of consciousness. It is a powerful method and can be used during analysis to integrate fantasies and images from the unconscious into the personality. The meaning and the moral demands that result are important. However, the active imagination should be used in the service of the conscious mind and be handled with care within the analytical framework and relationship. I write more about how such a work can be understood in Part II of this book. In *Jungian Psychoanalysis* (ed. Murray Stein 2010), both Jean Knox and Linda Carter write about how the transcendent function can be related to attachment theory, developmental perspectives, and intersubjectivity in Jungian psychoanalysis. Claus Bruun and Lilian Otscheret are also contemporary Jungian psychoanalysts, who in the above-mentioned book write about the concept of dialogue both from the historical perspective and from that of present-day analytical psychology.

In the third part of the book, I tie the three theories together to enrich the understanding of the elliptical dialogue. Here I attempt to elucidate how some of the fundamental concepts of systems theory, as put forward by Gregory Bateson, the language theory of Ludwig Wittgenstein, and the analytical psychology of C.G. Jung are interconnected. A common aspect of these theories is the strong connection between the authors' spiritual and ethical interests as exemplified in their personal lives and their different individuation journeys.

In connection with systems theory, I describe Francisco Varela's and Humberto Maturana's understanding of the system of homeostasis and autopoesis (the self-maintaining chemistry of living cells) and how this can be applied to the fields of systems theory and sociology. Complex Adaptive Systems (CAS) form an interface with natural and social science. Linda Carter and Joe Cambray refer to this in their writings (Stein, 2010, in Chapter 19, *Countertransference and Intersubjectivity* by Linda Carter p.201). Cybernetics is the discipline used by Bateson to launch the theory of double-bind in communications in schizophrenic family systems. This can be seen as a border area between systems theory and analytical psychology. But the first connection is the profound influence that Jung's poetic text *Septem Sermones ad Mortuos* has on Bateson to the extent that he is able to transform and incorporate his theory of mind at the spiritual level. The second connection is that Bateson's and Jung's theoretical concepts stemmed from physics. This is most clearly expressed in Bateson's *Mind and Nature* and in Jung's essay *On Psychic Energy* and his Harvard lecture on instincts, 1936. Published in a symposium as *Factors Determining Human Behaviour* (Cambridge, 1937) and as *Psychological Factors Determining Human Behaviour* (CW 8, §§ 232-262), Wittgenstein's language theory, on the other hand, was developed by social constructionism, as presented by John Shotter (2008) in his book *Conversational Realities Revisited: Life, Language, Body and World*.

It is my hope that the journey through the text will make you feel that language can facilitate dialogical relationships and that the spiral movement of the elliptical dialogue leads to a shared experience. The book begins by describing the elliptical dialogue. This is followed by the symbol of the Greek god Hermes, who works in the liminal space of the elliptical dialogue. Hermeneutics is the mercurial element in the elliptical dialogue that makes it flow. Hermes is always present in the in-between spaces of the relational dialogical sphere and in the intrapsychic domain. Hermes-consciousness is familiar with the deep archetypal and mythological layers of the psyche and is at home in the mercurial dialogue that takes place in Jungian psychoanalysis and Jungian style supervision. With his mercurial energy, Hermes is both the weaver of and the woven in whatever emerges in the elliptical dialogue. Hermes is in fact a guiding symbol throughout the book.

VERMEER
Tomas Tranströmer (1931-2015)

No protected world...Just behind the walls the noise begins,
the inn is there
with laughter and bickering, rows of teeth, tears, the din of bells
and the insane brother-in-law, the death-bringer we all must
tremble for.

The big explosion and the tramp of rescue arriving late
the boats preening themselves on the straits, the money creeping
down in the wrong man's pocket
demands stacked on demands
gaping red flowerheads sweating premonitions of war.

In from there and right through the wall into the clear studio
into the second that's allowed to live for centuries.
Pictures that call themselves 'The Music Lesson'
or 'Woman in Blue Reading a Letter' –
she's in her eighth month, two hearts kicking inside her.
On the wall behind is a wrinkled map of Terra Incognita.

Breathe calmly...An unknown blue material is nailed to the chairs.
The gold studs flew in with incredible speed
and stopped abruptly
as if they had never been other than stillness.

Ears sing, from depth to height.
It's the pressure from the other side of the wall.
It makes each fact float
and steadies the brush.

It hurts to go through walls, it makes you ill
but is necessary.
The world is one. But walls...
And the wall is part of yourself –
we know or we don't know but it's true for us all
except for small children. No walls for them.

The clear sky has leant against the wall.
It's like a prayer to the emptiness.
And the emptiness turns its face to us
and whispers
'I am not empty, I am open.'

**From New Collected Poems (1997/2011) Tarset:
Bloodaxe Books Ltd. From For Living and Dead (1989)
Trans Robin Fulton.**

PART I
THE ELLIPTICAL DIALOGUE

1. The elliptical dialogue as a map for Jungian psychoanalysis

The Geographer 1668.
Jan Vermeer (1632-1675.)
Copyright Städel Museum - ARTOTEK

The Astronomer 1668.
Jan Vermeer (1632-1675.)
Copyright Peter Willi - ARTOTEK

To create maps in order to understand ourselves and where we are in the inner and outer world is a part of human activity. It is archetypal. The making of structures helps forming an orientation when chaos and confusion are present in life. In the two images from Vermeer both "the geographer" and "the astronomer" are busy drawing and calculating positions on the collective level.

When moving to the personal, professional and theoretical level of being in the psychotherapeutical experience, there is also a creation of maps. The presented map of the elliptical dialogue is an attempt to integrate systems theory and language theory into analytical psychology. It is rooted in clinical and theoretical experience, and this map derived from many sources. During incubation the perspective was made up from my own analysis, dreams, training, lectures and important experiences with patients. All these living experiences, like words and maps are moving and have an urge sometimes to make themselves present from the unconscious to the "not yet" conscious toward consciousness. The map of the elliptical dialogue has been on the move and journeying for quite some time and now is present; this is what it looks like:

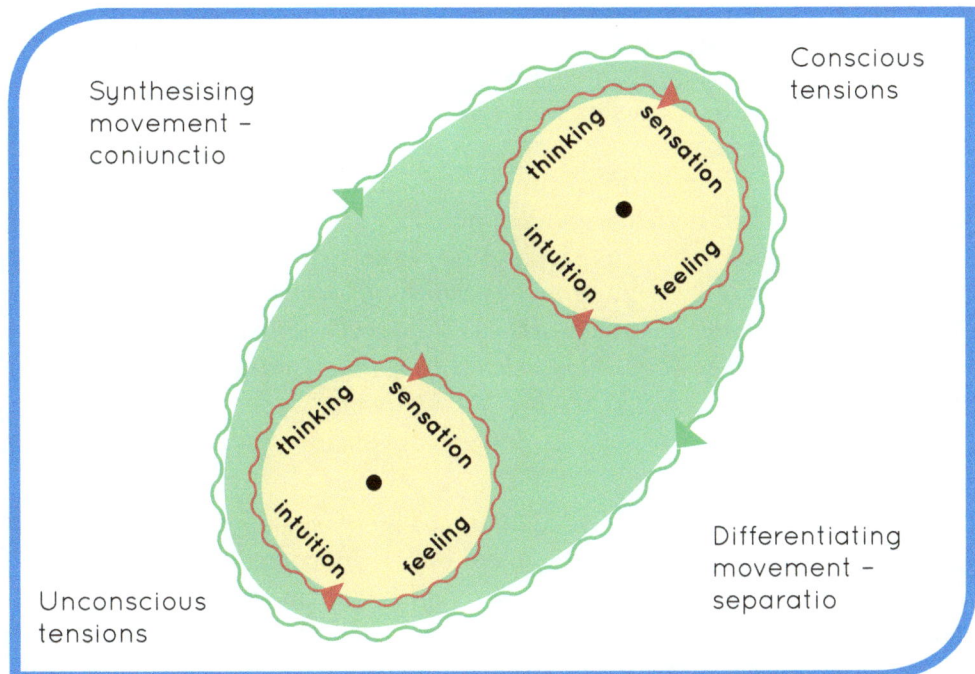

Figure 1. The Elliptical Dialogue – Figure Created by Gunilla Midbøe

The elliptical dialogue is both an image and a map for the clinical interaction that includes intrapsychic and interpersonal experiences within the setting of Jungian psychoanalysis and psychotherapy. It is a way of looking at and orientating oneself in the communication, the use of language, and the dialogue that are part of Jungian psychoanalysis.

In a broad sense, the term "dialogue" can be defined as a conversation between two or more people with the intention of exploring a subject—not with the aim of proving one's superiority over the other, but by listening carefully to the other within and other without and exchanging views. This skill was demonstrated long ago in Plato's dialogues, for example when Socrates proved to be a very good listener by reformulating what the other had said and reflecting it back. This reformulation is a kind of replacement or displacement of what has been said after careful listening. This is why in Plato's *Dialogues* the result is not a verbal duel, but a conversation that is skillfully crafted to pick up the intentions and tensions of the other, not by argument but by listening. From the very beginning, psychoanalysis used dialogue as a method. It was thus a therapeutic encounter at the level of words and language.

In a lecture titled "Principles of Practical Psychotherapy" given to the Zurich Medical Society in 1935, C.G. Jung acknowledged the relation between psychotherapeutic art and ancient philosophical discourse. He writes, "Psychotherapy is a domain of the healing art … (it is) a kind of dialectical process, a dialogue or discussion between two persons. Dialectic was originally the art of conversation among the ancient philosophers, but very early became the term for the process of creating new syntheses. A person is a psychic system which, when it affects another person, enters into reciprocal reaction with another psychic system" (Jung, 1935/1966, § 1). In the same opening paragraph of this address, Jung names two fundamental antinomies that are relevant to psychotherapeutic work: (1) "… *psyche depends on body and body depends on psyche.*" And (2) "… *the individual signifies nothing in comparison with the universal, and the universal signifies nothing in comparison with the individual.* There are, as we all know, no universal elephants, only individual elephants" (Jung, 1935/1966, § 1).

The implication of these fundamental tenets is spelled out in the next paragraph: "… since all life is to be found only in individual form, and I myself can assert of another individuality only what I find in my own, I am in constant danger either of doing violence to the other person or of succumbing to his influence. If I wish to treat another individual psychologically at all, I must for better or for worse give up all pretentions to superior knowledge, all authority and desire to influence. I must perforce adopt a dialectical procedure consisting in a comparison of our mutual findings. But this becomes possible only if I give the other person a chance to play his hand to the full, unhampered by my assumptions. In this way his system is geared to mine and acts upon it; my reaction is the only thing with which I as individual can legitimately confront my patient" (Jung, 1935/1966, § 2). This states the basic condition for genuine dialogue.

The interactive field of language and dialogue also has to be adjusted to an ethical attitude that preserves the integrity of both parties. In order to achieve integrity and respect for myself and for the other, it helps to think of the elliptical form as the shape of interactive movement within the analytical process. The elliptical dialogue is a map of the complexity of the interactive field that develops in psychoanalysis and its aim is to promote and sustain dialogic conversations. The elliptical dialogue is also relevant as a model for supervision in the Jungian style. Further, it can serve as a relational model for how to become aware of the specific dialogues and relational changes that take place in life cycle transitions in the individuation process in the first and second half of the life cycle. All these areas will be developed in what follows.

I use the adjective "elliptical" to describe a dialectical relationship between two people in a contained space, namely, within the analytic temenos, where temenos relates to the sacred and safe space for letting unconscious contents be brought into the light of consciousness. The root word, ellipse or ellipsis, refers to several different contexts. The word derives from the Latin *elleipsis*, which means "omission" or "leaving out." In literature, the term ellipsis is used to indicate an omission, such as when writing and leaving out what might commonly be understood from the context or what could be understood in different ways but is not yet accessible for understanding. In geometry, an ellipse is an oval with two centres. I use the term "elliptical" as a geometrical image in the form of a contained space with two centres, which designates the space in which a therapeutic dialogue can take place. This image serves as a map for considering the complexity of the therapeutic interaction at several levels and in a number of dimensions.

One can easily draw an ellipse as a geometrical form on a piece of paper with the help of a string and two nails. The length of the string will determine the size, and the distance between the nails will determine the shape of your ellipse. In drawing the elliptical form, the string has to be stretched around the two nails. Depending on the distance between the nails you can get a more circular or dilated, expanded ellipse.

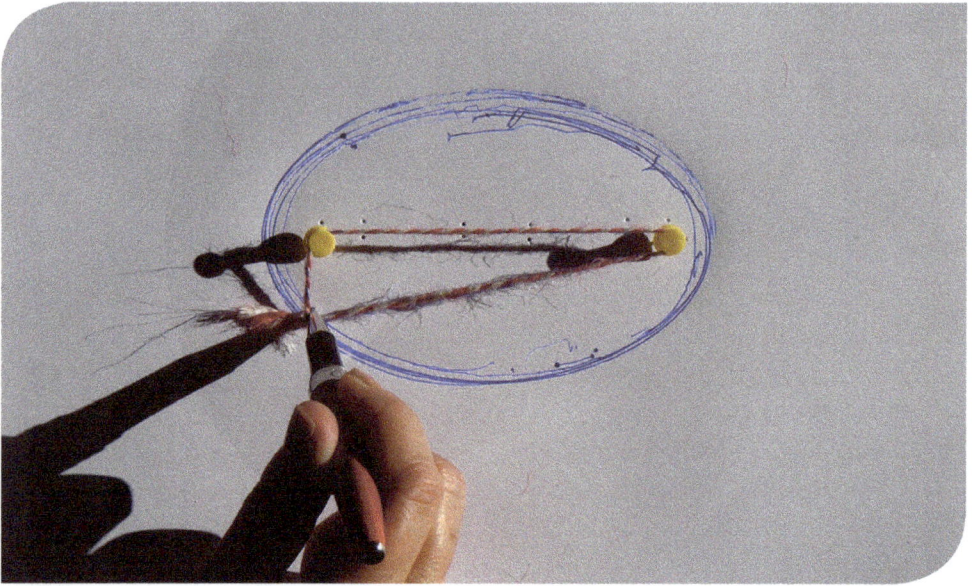

Figure 2. How to draw an ellipse - Photo by Lars Midbøe

As you can see here, the length of the string will determine the size, and the distance between the nails will determine the shape of the ellipse.

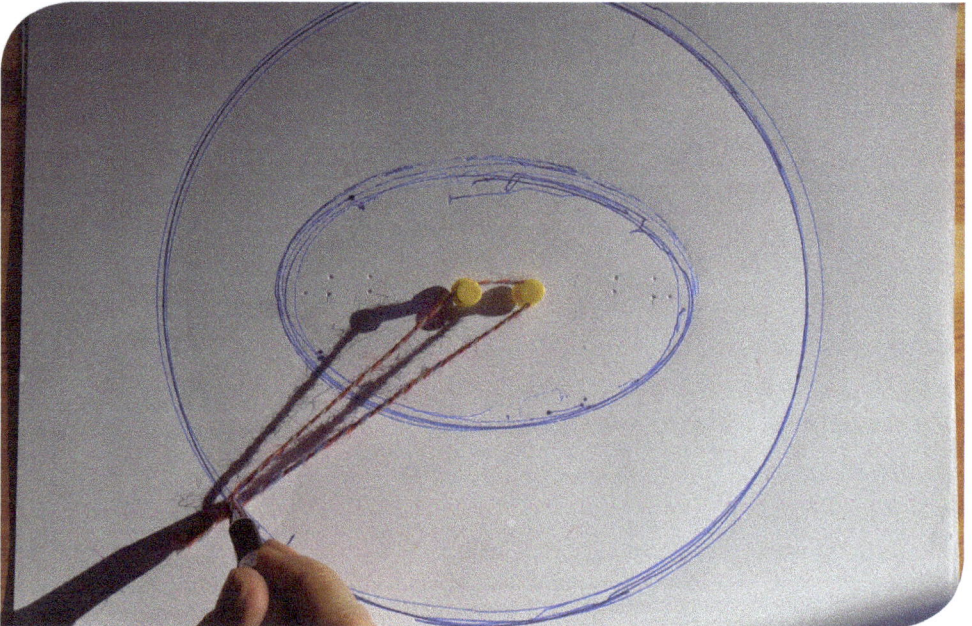

Figure 3. How to draw an ellipse - Photo by Lars Midbøe

In gardening, for example, this way of creating an elliptical flowerbed in large scale is often used.

In this book, the main focus is on the analytical exchange in all its dimensions. As seen in figure 1 (p. 21), the geometrical shape of the ellipse is "eccentric" in that it has two centres located at either end of an oval-shaped form. In the elliptical dialogue, each centre represents an individual in dialogue with the other centre (individual). Each individual is surrounded by a red circle with a black point in the middle, indicating the boundaries of each person's body and individuality. The black point at the centre of the red circle symbolizes the ego-self axis and its function in each individual. This dimension in the elliptical dialogue pertains to the internal communication dynamics that take place within each individual—an internal (intrapsychic) dialogue between the conscious and the unconscious level of that person.

A second dimension of the elliptical dialogue is the green ellipse surrounding the two red centres. The green ellipse is a dynamic line that runs in a clockwise direction. This dimension represents the language that is used between the participants and is referred to as the language dimension, in that it ties the two people together in spoken and nonverbal dialogue.

In this interpersonal dialogue, each individual has his or her own integrity and boundaries. This means that in the analytical session, three parallel dialogues take place at the same time: two internal dialogues indicated by the colour red in the above figure 1 (p. 21) and an outer or interpersonal dialogue coloured green. All three are contained in the analytical process as a whole, which is represented by the blue frame with two sharp and two rounded corners. This indicates that the agreed frame of the analytical work is flexible rather than rigid, but that it is still firm and not too open that it becomes vague and confusing.

The map of the elliptical dialogue can also be useful when looking at the everyday exchanges between people. For example, a friend of mine who is familiar with my work on the elliptical dialogue wrote this:

> On my walk this afternoon I saw the most marvellous example of an elliptical dialogue. A young mother with her 4-5-year-old daughter was walking on the trail ahead of me and I saw them speaking to each other. They were speaking in dialect so I didn't understand what they were saying, but they were obviously in a deep dialogue with each other. It was like playing tennis—the one spoke, then the other, back and forth, and with body language, a kind of swinging rhythm. Their

world was contained in the dialogue, and when I passed them I realized that the outer circle of the dialogue ellipse was intact—nothing came in from outside to disturb their communication flow, they were in their own language game, and what a beautiful sight it was. The mother broke the frame for a moment to greet me with a smile. I smiled back and passed on. As I passed, the ellipse closed, and they were back in their world intact. Words, body, gestures—a total communications package.

This brief episode from an afternoon walk belongs to the ongoing everyday stream of life. It shows the respectful exchange between people who recognize the value of flexible boundaries in relationships that are both intimate and impersonal, which maintains their integrity and the dialogue between them in different registers. I have reflected on this with regard to the different participant positions in the dialogue, the relational dynamics that take place between them and the protective shield that surrounds them, which seems to correspond with my diagram of the elliptical dialogue.

I use the map of the elliptical dialogue as a clinical tool to assess the kind of psychotherapeutic work that lies ahead and to help me take part in language interventions of ongoing psychotherapeutic work.

If we look at the elliptical dialogue from above, it looks flat, like a tabletop. As with a table, there is a space beneath the top and the legs. In other words, it is a three-dimensional form that can be twisted and turned from one side to the other. Seen from different perspectives, we can catch sight of the depth and dimensions of the dialogue. This following figure 4 illustrates what I mean.

It is important to keep this dimensionality of the ellipse in mind in order to capture the deeper resonances and associations of words used in the analytical setting and to become aware of what the words can trigger in each participant's psyche in the elliptical dialogue. This dimension runs from the deep unconscious layers connected to archetypal images in the "self field" in the participant's inner and outer reality, through cultural and personal complexes to everyday cognitive ego function exchanges.

It is also important to realize that the model can be in dynamic movement and even benefit from this seeming instability as long as the frame remains intact. To keep a state of balance while in constant movement resembles the feat of a tightrope walker, but the poles holding the rope upright cannot differ too much in height. This constantly balanced position, even when in

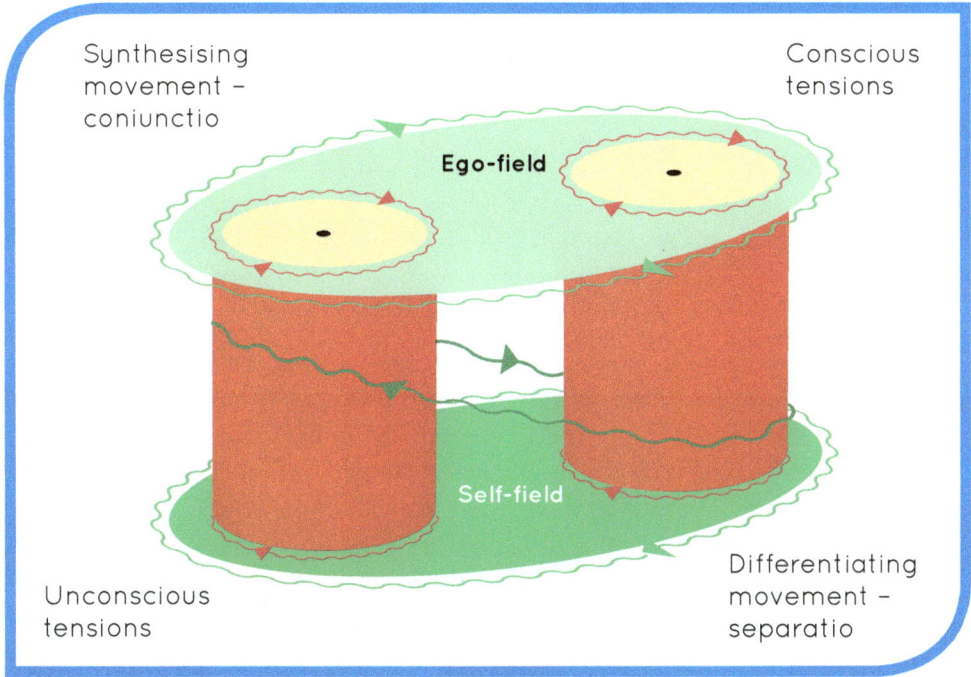

**Figure 4. The Elliptical Dialogue in depth dimension -
Figure Created by Gunilla Midbøe**

movement, keeps one from falling into the abyss or rupture and thus breaking the frame. The red cylinders with the black poles, seen from above as a red circle with a black point in the middle in the first diagram, are both a precondition for change and for the creation of an interpersonal relationship in the elliptical dialogue.

In practical terms, in a therapeutic session it is important to maintain a dynamic tension between the two centres of the ellipse. A delicate balance needs to be struck between confirming and challenging analysands. If confirmation becomes routine in the dialogue, there will be too little tension and hence little opportunity for new insights and development. If the poles get too close and the ellipse risks becoming a circle, a static state results with no "swing." In the ongoing dialogue, the elliptical green line — the string enclosing the psychotherapeutic exchange — has to be stretched in order to create a dynamic ellipse and the distance and closeness between the two individuals has to be carefully calibrated in each session. Moreover, the stretched string that forms the ellipse surrounding the two individual ego-self centres must stay within the blue frame. The stretching movement can be related to the arousal of curiosity in the constantly active energetic system of libido or psychic energy in both participants.

Patients often stimulate our curiosity from the moment they start to talk. In this way, they invite us to participate in more than just one new path of dialogue. It is our responsibility as psychotherapists to choose which of these invitations to accept. My experience is that it is best to accept one invitation at a time. If the string is stretched too much, it will break the frame. On the other hand, if the points are too close together, the dialogue will be circular and static, which will also break the dynamic elliptical rhythm and movement.

I think that our choices as psychotherapists need to be guided by an awareness of the ego-self axis within ourselves. In the diagram, this is indicated by the black circle inside the red cylinder. The connection and relationship between the ego and the self are a fundamental Jungian psychoanalytical concept that Erich Neumann developed following the theory of C.G. Jung. The space, or axis, between the ego and the self can be imaged as an upwardly spiralling path from the darkness of the unconscious self to the light of ego consciousness. The development of the transcendent function in this ego-self space enables the psyche to rhythmically walk up and down the path. The experience of moving from the self to a conscious ego position and from ego to self is the human psyche's way of allowing for creativity and freedom.

From this position, our choice of language and words as psychotherapists also depends on our introverted-extraverted personalities and being guided by how we, with our rational (thinking-feeling) and our irrational (sensing-intuitive) functions, perceive the spoken words and the language. Finally, with this constellation of ego-self space and the transcendent function within ourselves, we can put our reflections into words and thereby contribute to the green dialogical ellipse on the map. At the same time, we need to be open to other invitations from our clients and make the next choice of dialogical response. Words thus trigger all these complex levels, from the unconscious space under the table to the conscious tabletop surface. This corresponds to C.G. Jung's results from the Word Association Experiment (WAE) and to his image of the pattern of the transference relationship known as the marriage quaternity (Jung 1946/1981: § 422-425). From the beginning of Jung's clinical experience (Jung 1907 § 78-80, CW 3), affects played a major role in the forming of the personality and the different complexes that can hold us prisoner. Words trigger the affect-charged complexes in us and produce anxiety, inner sensations of discomfort and uneasiness, which in turn show themselves in our actions and behaviour. In a footnote (Jung 1907 § 80/4 CW 3) Jung compares this to leitmotifs in music:

This behaviour can be directly compared with Wagnerian music. The leitmotif, as a kind of feeling-tone, denotes a complex of ideas that are essential to the dramatic structure. Each time one or the other complex is stimulated by what someone does or says, the relevant leitmotif is sounded in one of its variants. It is exactly the same in ordinary psychic life, where leitmotifs are the feeling tones of our complexes and our actions and moods are modulations of the leitmotifs.

The more distinctly we are able to see conscious connections between the triggers and the affects, the more we are able to free ourselves for creativity and growth. We then become able to listen to our leitmotifs and, from a conscious ego position, choose actions and behaviour that reflect our specific, unique, individuation journey rooted in the self-field. In other words, it is akin to following the ego-self path from darkness to light, and vice versa. In contemporary research, this corresponds to what the American developmental psychologist Edward Tronick (2007) calls the unique relationship created by the therapist and the patient that makes the growth of new consciousness possible. This comes into being through the mutual regulation of affects.

In the Jungian psychoanalytical field, this regulation of affects is seen as a relational interplay that takes place simultaneously within and between individuals in liminality with language, body, and image. This transforms meaning and generates new perspectives. The transcendent function shows itself both as an intrapsychic and interpersonal power. With this in mind, I suggest a three-dimensional map of the elliptical dialogue that includes past, present, and future time perspectives—quantitative Chronos time—and nonlinear time perspectives—qualitative Kairos time.

In the above figure 4, the forms are made up by the ellipse, the circle, and the quarternity moving together in various constellations. These constellations are contained within the blue frame and the green elliptical dialogical form and hold the liminal space of the analytical relationship. The phenomenon that emerges in this context is various, which includes dreams, images, language, and bodily sensations. Within each of these, we find the tension of opposites. The elliptical dialogue as a map and a way of seeing and being in the analytical relationship brings symmetry and reciprocity to the analytical relationship, opens up a new territory of consciousness in the relationship and puts the focus on mutual responsiveness and reciprocity in the encounter.

These two maps of the elliptical dialogue facilitate entry to the model. In what follows, the blue frame, the black point surrounded by the red circle as ego-self connection, the green elliptical line of language and the energized hermetic and hermeneutic field of the white area are both deepened and explained. This is initially done using brief, small clinical vignettes of the analytical work that Björn and I developed and by then applying the biographical and theoretical aspects of C.G. Jung, Ludwig Wittgenstein, and Gregory Bateson.

THE BLUE FRAME — THE STORY OF A BEGINNING

On Monday afternoon at two minutes to 3 in the afternoon, the doorbell rings. I open the door to my practice, and he enters.

We had agreed on a session for our first meeting. He had called two weeks earlier saying, "I think I need to see a psychotherapist. There is so much going on inside me, and I have a dream that will not leave me."

From the moment we met, thoughts and feelings began circulating in our different inner and outer realities. He had called for help, and I had responded. As a psychotherapist, supervisor, and Jungian psychoanalyst, I may have been hooked by him saying: "I have a dream that will not leave me." This addressed the free space in my inner world that was open to a new analytical journey with the other individual. It also meant that my personal and professional experience of myself had to be open to change. I knew, too, that I needed to feel intuitively that the other person had the capacity to listen to deeper symbolic layers within the psyche. I may have picked up this intuitive feeling from Björn when he telephoned me. In Jungian psychoanalytical terminology, both of our self-fields were probably ready to open up and engage at a deep unconscious level, as indicated in the three-dimensional map of the elliptical dialogue (p.27). There, the self-field can be imagined as an unconscious, unknown energetic field that is constellated by each participant's self-field in the given analytical relationship. In short, we embarked on an analytical journey and opened the blue frame in the elliptical dialogue map.

AT FIRST LIGHT

"The blue hour is the period of twilight each morning and evening when the sun is a significant distance below the horizon and the residual, indirect sunlight takes on a predominantly blue hue. This effect is caused by the relative diffusability of short blue wavelengths of light versus the longer red wavelengths. During the blue 'hour' (typically the period is about 40 minutes in length), red light passes straight into space while blue light is scattered in the atmosphere and therefore reaches the earth's surface." (Wikipedia.)

The concept of the "blue hour," 40 minutes in length, is not quite an analytical hour but can nevertheless be applied to the blue frame and the context of the analytical work as it began to unfold between Björn and myself. Many processes take place at the same time. In this twilight time it is also important that issues relating to fees and timescales are clear. On the map of the elliptical dialogue the blue frame has sharp and rounded corners, which indicates that the frame is not rigid and self-sufficient but has to be flexible and adapt to the prevailing conditions. It also has to be able to contain strong feelings and actions. It can be seen as the vessel in which transformation takes place. At the same time, it must be a place of safety and security for the analytical relationship. In analytical psychology, this vessel is often imagined as the hermetic vessel used by alchemists for the transformation of the psyche and matter. The blue frame does not only refer to the outer facts and conditions for analytical work, but also serves to give the participants an inner sense and feeling that there is space and form for unconscious powers. This manifests itself as hints that ignite sparks of hope and curiosity and activate the neuronal "seeking system" (Solms and Turnbull, 2002 p. 202 and 210) and curiosity in both participants.

The analyst, psychotherapist or supervisor is responsible for the creation of the blue frame's conditions. In deep analytical work such as that entered into by Björn and myself, four areas of questions need to be reflected upon for my own inner dialogue and assessment of our work:

1. Is there an inner experience within the patient of a subjective suffering and pain? This area of reflection includes how the pain in the patient's life has been more or less felt and visible. It also refers to the underlying development of events and consciousness that connects to the final decision for making an appointment in present time.

2. Is there a wish for deeper self-knowledge? This area of reflection refers to the curiosity for a deeper self-knowledge. It includes the assessment of how symbols and inner images can be held and tolerated in the inner reality and become a source for development. Relief from anxiety and symptoms can be important for managing everyday tasks, but at the same time this area points to the client's readiness for the symbol to be taken care of and given meaning.

3. The third area includes the ability to get involved in analytical work over time. To address this area is about giving time and being committed to giving space in inner and outer reality to the analytical journey. This is not only about keeping agreements and timescales, but also being able to continue even when feeling uneasy, bad, empty, or angry, or if something else more interesting comes along to distract one's attention.

4. The fourth area of reflection has to do with trust. How can I as a therapist get a sense of the patient's ability to trust or his or her ability to risk trusting the analytical relationship? Trust is a big and crucial issue in a person's life and has often been challenged and misused in early childhood. Therefore, this fourth area is more about whether the person applying for psychotherapy is able to trust the analytical relationship. Here it is important to explore whether the analytical relationship has the potential to develop into deep analytical work that engages the symbolic levels of the psyche and at the same time allows the person under analysis to keep the core of the ego-function in check so that everyday tasks can be performed. If you are a parent with small children, it is important to give them care and security, but if you are a middle-age person with a fairly stable life situation, your degree of tolerance for anxiety might be greater due to no longer having any direct responsibility for your children. On the other hand, deep psychotherapeutical work with parents of small children can be very beneficial, not just for adults but also for children, in that children benefit from having parents who are more conscious of themselves. This core in the ego function is also important for how the analysand is able to reflect on the analytical relationship and cope with any anxiety that might be evoked. In analytical terms, this means working as harmoniously as possible without causing splits and separations in the analytical relationship. However, this is easier said than done, as we shall see in the clinical section of the book. Psychoanalysis and psychotherapy always include ruptures of some kind—from painful breaks of boundary to moments of numinosity. These ruptures can occur as sparks of light and hope from the deepest layers of psyche, but also as strokes of lightning that can shatter the vessel of analysis.

One of the important contributions of Jungian analytical psychology to the space inside the blue frame is that it points toward a field beyond our actual life situation as human beings that needs to be taken account of when considering analytical work. This field includes the self, the ego, and their mutual interconnectedness, how they separate and how they unite. As the moderator of the dialogue, the analyst needs to be able to hold these things together, contain them, and both separate and hold together the ego and the self. The ego-self axis constitutes the ground from which the analytical work springs. Together they make up the centre and the circumference of the human psyche. Using the concepts of ego and self, Jung creates both a perspective and a possibility beyond individual neuropsychology and cognitive theory. In the psychoanalytical work of our field, we can see how the ego, the self, and their interconnectedness are manifested in dream images, in the active imagination, and in the development of symbols used in clinical work. Jung defined the ego and the self in his major work *Psychological Types* (1921/1981.) Later in life he wrote *Mysterium Coniunctionis* (1955/1981), in which his major concern was to understand how the psyche coped with and overcame the inherent polarities of its energy. The synthesising movement of uniting opposites within the psyche created the necessary conditions for the individuation process.

When Björn walked into my practice, he also brought with him an image from the dream that would not leave him. (See illustration, part II p. 105 *The Rottweiler*.) He walked into the room with powerful steps and an expression of determination and fear in his eyes. He was eager to tell me about the dream and was just as eager to hear my interpretation of it. His hands trembled as he held his drawing of the dream. As our first session proceeded, with an exchange of words, body sensations, and agreements on time and further sessions, I felt that it was important to make the blue frame as clear as possible. This work involved a connection for us both—a connection that was grounded in the narrative of his dream and, especially, the word "fearful." I said something about him looking around the room to see whether the colours, furniture, sculptures, carpets, windows, and light could be a containing space for our dialogue and relationship. Whether it could be a safe place and space for him, where he could share his past and present "fear" and "fearful" experience with me. This was a way of connecting the blue frame, represented by the physical room and the imagined future dialogue, to our mutual and individual inner worlds of imagination.

On the map of the elliptical dialogue, the blue frame relates to inner, outer, physical, and psychic reality. The model as a whole can thus be used in different settings of reality and is not meant to be locked into the analytical room and its specific dialogue.

THE RED CYLINDER WITH THE BLACK POINT – THE STORY OF THE EGO – SELF AXIS

Before Björn and I sat down for our first Monday session, he gave me an image from his terrifying dream. He called it *The Rottweiler*. His body shook, and his hands trembled. "You keep it, and I hope it can stay here," he declared.

In the drawing, Björn and the Rottweiler dog stood close together. Björn's left arm held the dog in an upright position. Both of them faced forward and looked upward. The image indicated daylight. (See illustration Part II p. 105 *The Rottweiler*.)

"So you want me to keep the Rottweiler here for you?" I asked. "Yes, yes, and I also want you to interpret this dream," he said. A silence unfolded between us, and in that silence I remembered his voice on the telephone saying: "I have a dream that will not leave me alone."

I thought about Jung's writings in *A Study in the Process of Individuation* (Jung 1950/1968 CW 9i.). In his case study, Jung emphasises the importance of symbolic language and that it has to unfold in a way that takes irrational processes into account. The woman in the case, a Miss X, had come to Europe from the U.S.A. to visit and work with Jung in analysis. They had met in America during the 1920s, but at the age of 55 she felt she had "got stuck" and reached an impasse. She dreamed that she was caught and helplessly stuck in a rock, and in the background was the sea. In her dream she called for help and saw Jung in the guise of a medieval sorcerer coming toward her. He touched the rock with his magic wand and freed her. The rock instantly burst open, and she stepped out unharmed. She took an image from her dream (Jung 1950/1968 § 528 Picture 1) to her first session with Jung in October 1928, when they met again in Zürich. What Miss X wanted to know was what this liberation from the rock might mean for her in her life. In the transforming process of individuation that followed, she was fully liberated.

For me, as Björn's somewhat (at that moment in time) presumptive analyst, it was a question of both holding the image and letting it unfold—not by any rational plan and judgment, but by using my inner "eyes." It was as though Björn was fused with the dream image and imprisoned in this situation. My eyes saw Björn representing himself as a sphere. *The Rottweiler* image became a place for birth, and the image was Björn's first imprint of self. In the first hour of our work together, my function was to represent the light and consciousness to come. In Jung's case study of the Scandinavian woman (Jung CW 9i § 538), Jung talks about the analyst as the "precipitating" cause, which means that in the initial phase of analysis, the analyst can be likened to a meteor, with a tail of light streaming behind. In the case of Björn, his unconscious imaged itself in his essence of personality with instincts at work. Instinct is seen as the most original force of the unconscious and is expressed in face and body. Even though it may seem as though I was there by chance, and as a "precipitating cause," in fact I was there to meet him in a role that he had already projected. I felt from the beginning that he had high expectations of our time together. When preparing for my supervision, I saw the following image in my inner reality:

I saw myself holding a persona mask of the analyst before my eyes and looking at Björn through the mask. At the same time, albeit in different time intervals, our eyes met without the mask, in a kind of peekaboo gaze—a bit like interacting with a child, when playing. As the child grows older and begins to play with other children, this interaction turns into a game of hide-and-seek.

This fantasy image served as a bridge to his extreme sensitivity and impatience. At the same time as having unrealistic transference expectations with the Jungian-analyst-persona-mask, he could not stand the professionality the mask stood for, or me not being more real for him in the sense of giving a concrete form to a mother, mistress, and wife. He also talked about his oscillations between Björn alfa and Björn omega without anything to hold together and apart his ego-self. He said, "I am either Björn alpha or Björn omega with no letters and alphabet in between for creating a narrative that is bearable as my own life story."

As might be imagined, the task of balancing these tensions without too many hazardous ruptures was difficult. The creation of a floating peekaboo sight of connectedness was a challenge. I somehow had to balance my own active imagination of the peekaboo game and Björn's own imagining of Björn alpha and Björn omega without an alphabet in between that symbolized his early state of being — like the baby who had not yet connected to language. For myself as his analyst, I felt as though I was a mother relating to her baby at the beginning of its development. This preverbal experience of self is the nonverbal interplay—the dialogue—between parent and child. It is the profound mother tongue and native language for all children. Peekaboo is something that promotes relationship and builds words and language. Voice and body come together and form a necessary whole. I am here, I am not here, I am present, I am absent, I go away, and I return. The aim is to create a balance that permits the self-regulating field to work from within the psyche within the safety and security of a consoling relationship.

When Jung reflected on the case of Miss X, whom he had already met, he had a feeling and sense of her personality and background. He described her like this:

"As the daughter of an exceptional father, she had various interests, was extremely cultured, and possessed a lively turn of mind. (…) Her animus was not of the kind to give her cranky ideas. She was protected from this by her natural intelligence and by a remarkable readiness to tolerate the opinions of other people. (…) Since her relation to her mother left very much to be desired, as she herself realized, the feeling had gradually grown up in her that this side of her nature might have developed differently if only the relation to her mother had given it a chance. In deciding to go to Europe, she was conscious that she was turning back to her own origins and was setting out to reactivate a portion of her childhood that was bound up with her mother." (Jung 1950/1968 § 525.)

This excerpt from the case study clearly shows Jung's evaluation of how Miss X's ego and self functioned. This was a woman with a lot of self-confidence who was determined to continue her individuation journey toward consciousness. Her ego-self axis could hold and develop toward a more and more integrated and centering of her personality. Jung also commented on her ability to tolerate different opinions, i.e., that she could stand tensions in the analytical relationship without falling into negative transference and break the frame. I imagine that the relationship between Miss X and Jung developed in a way that allowed her own self to develop — not in the sense of being freed from dynamic tensions, but in the sense of being able to devote herself to their mutual psychoanalytical experience. On her last trip to Jung in May 1938, she produced what became image 24 in the case study. The image is titled "Night-blooming Cereus," which is a kind of cactus that is also called the Queen of Night. It rarely blooms, but when it does, it is at night. And its perfume is divine.

When I recalled Jung's work with Miss X at the moment Björn entered with his dream image, there were similarities but also many differences. Miss X had a much more stable ego-self connection than Björn, whose ego-self had the potential to develop but was still in a very babylike state. Of course, I am not Jung, but as this image came to me shortly after my graduation as a Jungian psychoanalyst, I was perhaps struggling with and eager to develop my own Jungian professional identity and juggling with my own ego-self position without idealizing C.G. Jung too much. I had crossed the threshold of professional individuation with my unique conditions and experience of life. When Björn left at 10 minutes to 4 on that first afternoon, I looked at the dream image again and sat with it for a long time. The two figures of Björn and the dog seemed so tight and close. The image imparted a feeling of tenderness between them, and I thought it was a good sign that they both stood upright on two legs, even though it was unnatural for a dog with four. It was as though the animalistic energetic field of instincts had to be close as a precondition for Björn's development. I also wondered whether it would be possible for them to change position to their respective natural physical states.

For Miss X and her imprisonment in the rock, and for Björn and his holding of the Rottweiler in an upright position, these situations appear to be irrational yet symbolic. Any further development of the image has to follow the eye and the vision of what is to come. Using the "eyes" allows us to enter into the irrational and the dream image and, with aid of language, formulate questions like: What do you see when you are holding the Rottweiler? What does the dog say to you? During the first hour with Björn, I could tell that he was familiar with dreams and symbols. The connection of his self-field with his everyday life situation sometimes seemed to overwhelm him. I became aware of an inherent but merged ego-self connection in his psyche, which was from time to time highly charged with instinctual affects.

The two factors that are involved here are reason and irrational instincts. Both of these operate within the red cylinder and the black point of ego-self. Instincts are biological in nature and enter our psyche as impulses and affects. Reason and will belong to the ego complex and to the decision-making and stand-point taking realm. These factors are also important when looking at the map of the elliptical dialogue and especially when focusing on the red cylinder with the black point as a pillar representing the ego-self axis and how they are connected and relate to each other in the axis. When looking at the two maps from their two perspectives it becomes clear that the red cylinder and black pillar are the foundation and the pillars that keep the table and the map of the elliptical dialogue in an upright and fairly balanced position.

Now we will look deeper into the concepts of ego and self and the transcendent function as they were first experienced by Jung and further developed by Erich Neumann (1905-1960).

JUNG'S DOORBELL RINGS ON A SUNDAY AFTERNOON IN 1916

The self is integral to the theory and practice of analytical psychology. For Jung, the fundamental archetype of the self expressed itself on a Sunday afternoon in 1916. In the years prior to this Jung had been fully absorbed in his inner world of emerging dreams and images and in the reading of Gnostic texts. This is also the period of confrontation with the unconscious described in his autobiography, *Memories, Dreams, Reflections* (Jung 1961/1989/2007) and that is outlined in *The Red Book* (Jung, ed. Shamdasani 2009.)

When the doorbell rang about 5 o'clock, the atmosphere in the house was tense. Jung had felt an inner energetic field emerge as a call to give shape to something, to formulate and express a kind of order from within. He was sitting near the door when the doorbell rang. When Jung opened the door, the house at 228 Seestrasse, Küsnacht, was suddenly filled with voices as if there was an invisible crowd present.

In *The Red Book* (2009), this encounter is described as a dialogue between Jung's I and his soul. His soul says: "They are here and will tear open your door." Jung expresses fear and the soul insists: "Let the dark ones speak." Later, the soul says: "Be quiet, or else you will disturb the work." Jung experienced the voices as the voices of "the dead coming back from Jerusalem where they found not what they sought." Following this, and over the course of three evenings, Jung wrote the poetic and special language of *Septem Sermones ad Mortuos*. The act of writing these sermons and formulating the language and words gave the numinosity of the archetype of the self shape and form. This is similar to what Björn did when he gave the Rottweiler dream colour and shape. Communicating to the outer world and to oneself by writing, drawing, or through gestures signals the beginning of an ego-self relationship and the activation of the transcendent function within the psyche.

Important pregnant words in *Septem Sermones ad Mortuos* are *Pleroma*, *Creatura* (in Memories, Dreams, Reflections), *Creation* (in The Red Book) and *Principium Individuationis*. These concepts are included in the first sermon, and in the *Red Book* the sermons are preached by Philemon (Jung's inner wise man) with his added commentaries and dialogue with the voices of the dead. In the text Philemon also dialogues with Jung's ego function and his soul I as a kind of clarification of the context and of the voices returning from Jerusalem. The voices of the souls on Jung's doorstep can be seen as unindividuated souls that have to return to the world in order to become part of a dialogue in which they can gain consciousness and understanding in order to enhance a more complete God image and to finally rest in peace. The dialogue between Philemon and the voices of the dead is full of strong feelings and affects. Like many inner voices they demand, shout, and are angry and clinging. In their transformative appearance, they do not give in until they are satisfied. In the last sermon, Philemon says: "Man is a gateway, through which you pass from the outer world of Gods, demons, and souls into the inner world"; and later: "But when Philemon had finished, the dead remained silent. Heaviness fell from them, and they ascended like smoke above the shepherd's fire, who watches over his flock by night." A peaceful and very imaginative scene thus unfolds before our eyes. Continuing reflections then appear as a meta-dialogue between Jung's I of his soul and Philemon: "But I turned to Philemon and said: 'Illustrious one, you teach that man is a gateway? A gateway through which the procession of the Gods passes? Through which the stream of life flows? Through which the entire future streams into the endlessness of the past?'" Philemon answers by saying: "These dead believed in the transformation and development of man."

Now—a hundred years later—when reading and reflecting on the text of the Sermons as it is appears in *The Red Book*, it is clear that here we have an entire reference to the theory of analytical psychology and its many different levels: from the deepest level of how the self (the voices waiting at Jung's front door) surfaces to the level of inner dialogue with Philemon as a mediating figure who can communicate with the voices and with Jung's soul I. Based on his own experience, Jung believed in the transformative power of human beings. In a letter to Joan Corrie dated February 29, 1919, on the Sermons, Jung writes this:

"The primordial creator of the world, the blind creative libido, becomes transformed in man through individuation & out of this process, which is like pregnancy, arises a divine child, a reborn God, no more (longer) dispersed into the millions of creatures, but being one & this individual, and at the same time all individuals, the same in you as in me …& in the last sermon you find the beginning of individuation, out of which the divine child arises…" (Jung The Red Book p 354 footnote 123.)

The text of *Septem Sermones ad Mortuos* also forms the basis of Gregory Bateson's theory of mind and nature, as we shall see later when connecting systems theory and analytical psychology. What struck Bateson most about this text was the transformative nature of mind and nature. This formed a connecting bridge that was fundamental to his concept of family systems theory and cybernetics.

This particular text also appears in *The Red Book*. The seven sermons preached by Philemon can also be found there. These sermons also serve as examples of elliptical dialogue. In these sermons, Jung's soul I and Philemon engage in an elliptical dialogue in the context of the blue frame, which forms the theory and practice of analytical psychology. In the first sermon Philemon says:

"Now hear: I begin with nothingness. Nothingness is the same as fullness. In infinity full is as good as empty… We call this nothingness or fullness, the *Pleroma*." "*Creation* is not in the Pleroma, but in itself… we are distinguished from the Pleroma in our essence as creation, which is confined within time and space. ... Differentiation is creation. ... Yet we need to speak about our own differentiation, so that we may sufficiently differentiate ourselves. ... Hence the creature's essence strives toward differentiation and struggles against primeval, perilous sameness. This is called the *principium individuationis*. This principle is the essence of the creature" (Jung The Red Book 2009).

So in the poetic language of Septem Sermones ad Mortuos (M,D,R 1961/1989/2007, The Red Book, 2009), we find the essence of the theory and practice of analytical psychology. The words pleroma, creatura (creation) and principium indviduationis (individuation) set the Jungian concept of the self in motion and form the red cylinder of the self on the map of the elliptical dialogue. The ego, and its will to respond, often creates an image of the dream (as in Björn's case) or a narrative (like Jung's). This allows the images and words that arise from the unconscious to be expressed. The red cylinder in the elliptical dialogue model represents the location of the ego. The locus of the ego may be concealed, but for the analyst it is important to see and connect to the central point. In Björn's case, his ego function was regressed. He behaved like a small boy and wanted me to take care of him in all kinds of ways—at the beginning of our encounter by the demand that I interpret his dream immediately. I responded by suggesting that I could keep the dream image in my practice for a while.

When our first session was over and he left my practice, I looked at his drawing of the dream, saw the two upright figures of Björn and the Rottweiler, and Björn's arm around the dog. Both their faces were close and parallel. For me, this indicated an imprint of Björn's self. In the centre, there was a locus of upright, forward movement and gaze. After Björn had accepted that my practice and our sessions could be places of security for him—the establishing of the blue frame—his ego-self axis was able to begin to move and establish like a little more solid pillar with an ego and I centre.

For Jung, this meant committing himself to communicating the fundamental pattern of *Septem Sermones* by ordering and interpreting its contents and developing the structure and theory of analytical psychology. One of his first metapsychological results was published in 1921 as *Psychological Types*. This is volume 6 in the *Collected Works of Jung* and is commonly referred to as his type theory and how to understand the structure of ego-consciousness, extraversion, introversion, and the four functions of thinking, feeling, sensation, and intuition. In his writings Jung points to the danger of using Psychological Types as a communication of labels. In order to really understand this book, Jung recommends that readers immerse themselves in

Chapters II and V in which he underlines the poetic language, the relationship between the individual and the other, and that the unconscious is just as real as the conscious outside world. In the theory of analytical psychology with the self as a transcendent cylindrical form, the black ego point is the epicentre. In 1921, Jung defined individuation as follows: "The concept of individuation plays a large role in our psychology. In general, it is the process by which individual beings are formed and differentiated; in particular, it is the development of the psychological individual (q.v.), as a being distinct from the general, collective psychology. Individuation, therefore, is a process of differentiation (q.v.), having for its goal the development of the individual personality." (CW 6, § 757)

On the map of the elliptical dialogue, these cylinders carry the entire construction. They are uneven in length in the sense that the analyst's ego-self axis is more oriented toward consciousness and also in the sense that the analyst has to assess the analysand's ego-self axis. When I saw Björn holding the Rottwieler close and tight, I realized that this was the potential space for development into consciousness and hope in times of despair and anxiety. It is important for the analyst to be able to form an inner image of how the analysand's ego-self axis is constructed and to place it in the relationship as one of the two centres within the green line of the ellipse. The other centre consists of the analysand's own ego-self axis. I thought that our work together would also be a challenging journey for me. This is, of course, one of the reasons for becoming a Jungian psychoanalyst and continuing to exchange my experience of analytical work with colleagues and mentors.

When Jung was confronted with his own unconscious, it was important to have a point of support in the outer world. For him, his family life and professional work served as anchors. He knew that he had a normal life and felt like an ordinary person. Jung's point of normal existence was in his family, his profession and his home at 228 Seestrasse, Küsnacht. This was important for holding together and apart the ego and the self-positions in the transcendent movement of analytical work. The self can thus be seen as the epicentre of analytical psychology. When it shows its presence, the ego is like a black needlepoint that indicates the direction of a person's individuation journey.

ERICH NEUMANN AND THE EGO-SELF AXIS

One of the most talented and interesting analytical psychologists to develop analytical psychology from the fundamental concepts of C. G. Jung is Erich Neumann (1905-1960). Born in Berlin in 1905, he left his native Germany in 1933 and studied with Jung in 1934 and 1936. From 1934, his permanent home was Tel Aviv. After World War II, he was able to return to Europe and the Eranos Conferences became places where he could develop his thinking in dialogue with other scholars and scientists. After C. G. Jung's retirement in 1951, Neumann became the main lecturer at the Eranos summer seminars in Ascona, Switzerland.

I received a copy of *Amor and Psyche, The Psychic Development of the Feminine, A Commentary on the Tale by Apuleius* (1956) about 30 years ago. This was my main entrance into analytical psychology. I did not know then that Erich Neumann, the author of that essay, was a Jungian psychoanalyst. This text helped me to understand more about gender perspectives from both a developmental and clinical point of view. I think that Neumann structures and conceptualizes analytical psychology. He is exciting and points toward ways of integrating the feminine perspective into our patriarchal world. He also develops female animus psychology and male anima psychology. For me, his relational perspective became the bridge to a more holistic systems theory and an anchor in depth psychology. Just as I consider Jung's poetic text *Septem Sermones ad Mortuos* to bridge the borderlands between analytical psychology and systems theory, Neumann's essay on Amor and Psyche bridges systems theory and gender-specific developmental depth psychology. Both texts have a numinous character and as such are symbols for the cross-fertilization of systems theory, language theory, and analytical psychology. The relational nature of the three theoretical paradigms make them suitable for fruitful and synthesizing elliptical dialogues, as will be presented in the integrative Part III of this book.

Neumann worked on the ego-self axis in both his writings and practice (Neumann 1954, 1955, 1956, 1973, 1989, 1994). This concept forms the basis of his major meta-psychological essay called *The Psyche and the Transformation of the Reality Planes* (1989/1952). This is the first essay in *The Place of Creation* (Neumann 1989), which contains the lectures he gave at Eranos Conferences from 1952 until August 1960, four months before his death at the age of 55. In this text he creates a map and explains the position of humanity and especially our psychic personality in the world. He talks about field-knowledge as extraneous knowledge that is present and emergent in the living field. The map that Neumann constructed (ibid. p. 19) can be seen as an epistemological map for his contribution to the development of analytical psychology:

"To begin we must consider the nature of the 'archetypal field' which contains the collective unconscious. In doing so we must clarify the transgressive character of this field in its metapsychical and its metaphysical structure. Then we must elucidate the alternative character of this field, a field which appears either as an effect of energy or as form (Gestalt). …In this context we must also consider the tritemporal nature of our conscious minds and the different orientation to time which seems to be characteristic of certain archetypal structures.

A further chapter ought to be devoted to the self-field, a regulatory field superior to the archetypal field. The connection between the self-field and the ego-consciousness is brought about, as I see it, by the self-ego and ego-self axis; namely, the central axis which constellates the regulating phenomenon of form and thereby the possibility of cognition per se.

Developments connected with the ego-self axis are part of the specific human nature, insofar as we differ from animals. They are closely bound up with the specifically human experiences of creativity and freedom." (ibid. Pp. 18-20.)

It is significant that the ego-self axis forms an energetic field that has the potential to contain the further development of creativity and freedom. Neumann emphasises that the axis itself constellates the regulating phenomenon of form and cognition. This means that if a person's axis is fused and more or less invisible, as I made the judgment with Björn, he or she can begin to build on it. This building process is crucial and takes the form of unconscious projective energy. When a client begins to see and perceive the ego-self axis in the therapist, something important begins to take place. The therapist's perceived ego-self axis within the patient can then be seen as a hope for development. This process takes place both in conscious and unconscious tensions within the white Hermes field of the elliptical dialogue. This is also the relational and dialogical bond within and between the client and the therapist and brings the elliptical dialogue at work in all its dimensions. This forms a hopeful and meaningful image for the client to cling to when hopelessness reigns.

In Neumann's interpretation of the mythological tale of Amor and Psyche, there is a decisive moment for Psyche. This happens when she is cut off from the relationship with Eros and he returns to his mother Aphrodite. Psyche falls naked to the ground, all alone, pregnant and without protection, attachment and relationship. She is in a suicidal state and wants to throw herself in the water. Pan, the god of nature, sees her and gives her hope by clearly holding his own ego-self axis. He says something like, "No, no, life is not without hope, don't throw yourself into the water, remember you are pregnant and you can go and find the path of love. That is where you can put your energy into the quest of finding your own path guided by love itself." Psyche listens and crawls up naked to the shore to continue her individuation journey. This is why it is important for psychotherapists with a Jungian identity to have inner images of their own ego-self axes and how they communicate and form a relationship with their clients' ego-self energetic system. This enables the client to see and connect to the analyst's ego-self axis as a necessary lifebuoy in times of despair and self-devaluation, when the energetic field is free-floating in a chaotic and pleromatic state. This, I think, is valid for psychoanalytical work and for Jungian consultation and supervision.

Returning to Björn's symbolic image of his self-field with himself and the Rottweiler dog in an upright position, combined with his ego claims on me to fulfill his wishes for an immediate interpretation of the dream, I could sense his pressure. It was really like the pressure on a child who was at risk of becoming overwhelmed. In such a case, the task becomes one of training but not taming the ego-self function. At the beginning of our analytical work the imbalance of our respective ego-self axes was obvious, and I had to be creative and flexible without blurring boundaries and frames. When the energy from Björn's self-field was set free to express itself within the map and container of the elliptical dialogue, it was able to open up to an overwhelming and almost explosive energy. Floods like this have to be contained and taken care of by the transcendent function of the spiral path. The inner pathway begins from the self-field and reaches the ego-field of the psyche. When you can sense, follow, and begin to get a feeling of the path, it becomes a psychic link or spinal cord that can also be understood as the transcendent function. As I see it, this vertical, horizontal and hermeneutic movement comes into being when the individual psyche pays attention to dreams and fantasies and is able to put them into words, dialogue, and language on the elliptical dialogue map. In analytical psychology, this forming of the relationship between ego and self that consists of the axis is created by active imagination. Active imagination as a method is one of the cornerstones of Jungian psychoanalytical work. For Björn and myself, the work of forming a relationship within and between ourselves began already in the first few minutes of our first session and continued to develop when he began to tell me about his dream. The act of telling and telling within a dialogue forms the content of the green elliptical movement where language in all dimensions reside.

THE GREEN ELLIPSE—THE STORY OF A PREGNANT WORD

I invite Björn to take a seat. We sit down face-to-face. I hold *The Rottweiler* image in my hands. He tells me about his dream:

> "I'm standing in a garden, in the sunlight, and it's daytime. I am holding the Rottweiler dog close to me, I can even feel his cheek next to mine and his breath. It's an exhausting and fearful position to be in. And the Rottweiler says in a distinct voice: 'If you only stand still, nothing will happen...'"

Björn was terrified when he narrated the dream. It was as though he was inside the dream and experiencing it all over again. The complex of fear held him in a position in which his ego-self axis (the black point in the red circle) was in limbo.

The green elliptical line on the map of the elliptical dialogue represents the words and silences that are exchanged in an analytical session. Here, the most important aspect is how the words and expressions exchanged in the elliptical dialogue form a mutual and reciprocal relationship. Language enables us to enter into a relationship with in different ways and helps us to express our inner truths. The relational capacity of language creates the dynamic configurations of words, silences and sentences in the analytic dialogue. In this sense, words can be said to be pregnant with meaning. They have an aura around them that is specific to the given context. However, it is also important to use words carefully so that they do not confuse, reject, or are experienced as a verbal box on the ear.

The first pregnant word to enter the relationship between Björn and myself was **fearful** ("… It's an exhausting and **fearful** position to be in. And the Rottweiler says in a distinct voice: 'If you only stand still, nothing will happen…'). If my memory serves me correctly, I began by asking him when he had this dream. I also entered into the dream image by asking what he could **see in the words he used** when recounting the dream: "What do you see in the **word fearful**?"

Björn then told me the story of an authoritarian upbringing in a wealthy family during World War II. His father's family had owned an ironworks but had lost their position and money during the economic depression of the

1930s. His father was a repressive force, and his mother was mentally unstable: "She was a neurotic bundle of nerves." When Björn was too enthusiastic about something, he was shut up in a wardrobe, in the dark, alone, but with a tiny window through which he could see the moon. This was his primal experience of fear. In my own inner dialogue, I realized that I had to stay close to what "fearful" meant for Björn from a number of different perspectives. I invited him to look at the word "fearful": "Björn, I hear you say 'fearful.' If you and I, sitting here now, look into that word, what does it show us?" This invitation brought us, in our green ellipse, to a deeper structure of what the word "fearful" meant for him and for us in our analytical work.

> "I grew up without a mother and a father; for me, that meant that I have had and still have great difficulties in orienting myself in this world. Every afternoon when father returned from his office, we three brothers had to line up in front of the threshold to the dining room before entering for dinner. We were inspected and were almost never approved without remarks. Who am I beyond these scrutinies? Where is myself -- Björn?"

In many respects Björn showed himself in my practice. He used the room (seen as part of the blue frame) and our relationship in his eagerness when giving me drawings, which he hoped that I would like. And I really did. They expressed strong feelings and important motives in our work. He was also very dependent on what I thought about him and wanted to behave well. On the other hand, like all children, he tested the boundaries by wanting me to be more personal in my relationship with him: "It is not fair that I know almost nothing about your life. And you know so much about me." At one level, he understood the blue frame and the conditions for analysis. However, at another level, his ego found it difficult to cope with these conditions. The words his ego used were not those of an adult. This also reflected the location of his ego function. He did not disguise himself, which I regarded as a creative factor within the green elliptical line of our dialogue. On the map of the elliptical dialogue the green elliptical line is the point of observation where it is possible to find the areas that can be entered and exited with the stories of one's life. This is central to all encounters in the context of psychotherapy. The green elliptical line should be kept integral and move in accordance with the participant's ego-self axis. This concern for integrity and movement is the responsibility of the psychotherapist in that it forms the fuel for the ego-self axis, for consciousness, and for individuation. The relational language and dialogic words that inhabit the green elliptical line are therefore worthy of attention and illumination.

LUDWIG WITTGENSTEIN'S BRICK IN NORWAY AND IN LANGUAGE

I am holding a small brickstone in my hand. It is light in colour, with a rough, uneven surface on one side of it and a smooth glossy surface on the other. One side is covered with soot from Wittgenstein's fireplace in his cottage in Skjolden. Ludwig Wittgenstein (1889-1951) visited Norway for the first time in September 1913, together with his friend from Cambridge, David Pinsent. They arrived by boat from England to Christiania (now Oslo) and continued by train to Bergen. The tourist office arranged accommodation for them in Øystese, Hardangerfjord. For Wittgenstein, it was very important to be alone and not meet tourists. According to Pinsent (Vatne 1991, Monk 1990), Wittgenstein had never had such a successful holiday. They stayed for three weeks, and at the end of the stay Wittgenstein concluded that he wanted to settle down in a place where he could work in peace without disturbance from the outer world. On his return to Cambridge, he told his friend and mentor, Bertrand Russell (1872-1970) about this decision. In a letter to Lucy Mary Donnelly dated 19 October 1913, Russell writes that Wittgenstein entered like a whirlwind after returning from Norway and promptly stated that he wanted to settle down there and live in solitude until he had solved all the problems with logic (Monk 1990). Russell thought that this was a crazy idea and warned him about the dangers of solitude. At the same time, Russell was determined to draw out Wittgenstein's thoughts and help to formulate them in language. As a result of Wittgenstein's desire for silence and solitariness, he finally acquired a cottage in Skjolden in the innermost Sognefjord called Lustrefjorden, which had been recommended to him by the Austrian consulate general in Bergen, Kroepelin. It seems somewhat paradoxical that Wittgenstein chose Skjolden for the peace, solitude, and silence that he regarded as essential for his work. At that time, Skjolden was a very active trading community and attracted many tourists. The English gentry in particular were very fond of the fishing there, while other tourists came to climb the mountains. It could be said that it was thanks to the intense activity that Wittgenstein came to Skjolden, but how did this fit with his need for solitude?

Perhaps we can think of Wittgenstein's need for a cottage in Skjolden as similar to C. G. Jung's need to build a tower in Bollingen as a place where thoughts and creativity could grow in silence in a liminal state, surrounded by a landscape connected to water. In Wittgenstein's case, he was also surrounded by a foreign language, although he is reported to have learned Norwegian rather quickly and that he was able to have basic conversations with the inhabitants of Skjolden (Vatne 1991). The winter of 1913-14 was a critical time in Wittgenstein's life. After visiting his mother in Vienna for Christmas, he returned to Skjolden in January 1914. He had also ended his relationship with Bertrand Russell, whom he regarded as being much too different and difficult to communicate with. They had in fact stopped discussing philosophy, music, and art long ago. Wittgenstein turned instead to G. E. Moore, another colleague from Cambridge, and invited him to Skjolden—or perhaps more accurately, demanded his presence: "You must come to visit as soon as the holiday is over," he wrote on 18 February. Moore found it impossible to refuse and stayed for two weeks. According to Moore, during this period Wittgenstein talked, and Moore listened and took notes while Wittgenstein dictated. These notes formed the basis of *Tractatus Logico-Philosophicus*, which was first published in 1921 under the German title of *Logisch – philosophische Abhandlung*. In 1922, it was released in England as a book, with the original German language and the English translation side by side. Bertrand Russell and George Edward Moore both acted as godfathers for the book.

Language and words in dialogue and narrative are fundamental for psychotherapy. Jung regarded the symbol as pregnant with meaning and pointed to the symbol as a transcendent force. We might think about the symbol as a dream image, a fantasy or an object that we are strongly attached to. The built-in force and power of the symbol can also be compared with Wittgenstein's view of language and words. In *Tractatus Logico-Philosophicus*, Wittgenstein is concerned about the structure of logic in language and, therefore, also with the limitations of language. In the very first sentence of *Tractatus*, Wittgenstein states that "the world is everything that is" (1) and then specifies that "the world is the totality of facts not of things present."(1.1) Wittgenstein's statement of things as secondary can mean that it is not the thing in itself that denotes the world, but the relationships in-between—in the same way that knowledge about the theory of atoms or the planets in the solar system is not very useful without knowledge about the powers that are active between the particles. It is thus the relationships themselves that create the dynamics of the system, because "objects are consistent and given, but the configurations are shifting and inconsistent, changeable." (Wittgenstein *Tractatus logico-philosophicus* 1961/1992, 2.0271.) Here, Wittgenstein presents a set of well-articulated and almost axiomatic formulations like bricks in his language theory. He advocates a serious view of the function of language and says that you have to be silent about the content that cannot be spoken about. If something can be said, he thinks that it should be said in a clear and distinct way. It is as if he tries to set up a distinct borderline in language between the meaningful and the anti-meaningful expressions of language, hence the last sentence in *Tractatus*: "What we cannot speak about we must pass over in silence." (7.) This is one brick in Wittgenstein's language philosophy. In the last of Wittgenstein's major work *Philosophische Untersuchungen/Philosophical Investigations* (1953), there is focus on the everyday use of language and the multiplicity of ordinary language. The voicing and intoning of our words matter here, and the use of language is compared to how to understand a theme in music (1953, no 527) or the way of paying attention to words' rhythm and pace when reading a poem. The word "language*game*" is introduced and points toward the speaking of language as a part of activity and form of life (1953, no 23.) This building block or brick is, together with the first one, of major importance in the whole construction of Wittgenstein's language philosophy.

Turning to the green line in the elliptical dialogue the pregnant words "fearful" and "fear" that Björn used then works as set of "signposts" staking out an individuation journey over a shared landscape where there are several possible places to go. Understanding words as poetry or music in this way is more like having the same attitude to the working in words that can call for further expectations and experiences within intrapsychic as well as interpersonal elliptical dialogues in an analytical journey. Wittgenstein concludes that the logical structures that are the precondition for language can be shown and emerge as images and voices. This again reminds us of the interactions between parent and child. This is a field in which Wittgenstein comes close to the essence of archetypal theory in analytical psychology. The archetypal image is an expression that comes about in dreams and symbols and, as such, is also an expression of the deeper strata and structures of our human mind and psyche. Jung and Wittgenstein meet each other here, I think. But within this silence and unknown area there is a more powerful, existential silence: "To an answer that is not possible to express there is a question that is also not possible to put forward." (Wittgenstein, 1961 no 6.5.) But it is possible to solve or rather dissolve the problems that are formulated. One of the interesting things about Wittgenstein's philosophy is that he differentiates between the world of facts, where the world of facts is given and should not be confused with ethics, aesthetics, and religion. The unspoken exists and it *shows* itself as the mystical (Wittgenstein, 1961 no 6.522.) He refers to this category as transcendental—the mystical world that is impossible to speak about in the language of mathematical logic. Hence, the two famous sentences:

"The limits of my language mean the limits of my world."

and

"What we cannot speak about we must pass over in silence."

(Wittgenstein, 1961 5.6 and 1961 7)

This last quote signals the end of *Tractatus Logico-Philosophicus*. But Wittgenstein could not leave the other world out of his own life or his philosophical work. World War I changed him dramatically as a human being. He donated all his money (some to poets like Rilke and Trakl by donating to the journal *Brenner*) and lived a simple life as a primary school teacher in the small community of Puchberg am Schneeberg in Austria. The British philosopher, mathematician, and economist Frank Ramsey (1903-1930) visited Wittgenstein here. Ramsey is described as easygoing, simple, and modest, and was instrumental in translating Wittgenstein's *Tractatus Logico-Philosophicus* into English. He also managed to persuade him to return to philosophy and Cambridge. Meanwhile, Wittgenstein's cottage in Skjolden had been made ready for him, and he returned there in 1921. Language as everyday language came to the fore, and he became more and more interested in the religious language of myths and legends and its significance as patterns of wisdom.

He asked himself, "What gives language life?" From this question he developed the term "language–game," in which talking, speaking, and language were part of an activity and a way of life (Wittgenstein 1992, 23). *Philosophical Investigations* (1953) was released after his death in Cambridge in 1951. In this text edited by Georg Henry von Wright, he takes language from the domain of mathematical logic to the domain of liminality and spirituality. Here he also writes about seeing in words and being able to hold a double perception in language that is more tuned into the language of poetry and music. This particular perspective of language has been a concern for many philosophers and is further developed in the social constructivist area of family therapy that I regard as a relational psychotherapy. Sociologists like Johan Shotter (1993), literature scientists like Michail Bachtin (1990) and the philosopher Gaston Bachelard (1932/2013, 1960/1971) are important followers of Wittgenstein's works. For me, their thoughts about language are interesting in that they all see dialogical communication as the sphere of life for us human beings.

This description of Wittgenstein's development of his theory of language is useful in relation to the green elliptical line on the map of the elliptical dialogue, because it helps us to order language to see the clear and dual perspective of what is said and can be said. This is our challenge in analytical dialogue, I think. Being able to find the dialogical words and hold the tension between opposites in language without shallow interpretations is important. When, in later life, Ludwig Wittgenstein wrote what was posthumously published as *Philosophical Investigations* (1953), his emphasis was on the changing aspects of language that can also change our lives in terms of the vertical and horizontal growth of the ego-self axis in individuation and for development aided by psychoanalysis, different kinds of psychotherapy, and clinical supervision in the context of psychotherapy.

The brick from Skjolden and from Wittgenstein's cottage are just as physical as words from one person to another and can be rough, smooth, hard, and penetrating. Just as in the elliptical dialogue, when we swing toward the levels and depths of increased consciousness that give us new possibilities in life. It brings to mind the childhood experience of digging tunnels in the snow or sand and hand meeting another hand from the other side of the tunnel. At this moment, the sand or snow melted away and the touch of fingertips and hands opened a new shared world of a new reality that prior to that had been Terra Incognita.

As we will see in the clinical Part II, Björn's word **fearful** was one of the first dialogical words we used together. This word formed the first tentative building block of our dialogue, and from this developed the creation of the relationship and movement in the contained ego-self sphere within and between us. Thus, dialogue becomes the magnetic field that forms and holds the analytical work; not in a mechanical way, but in a way that stays open to the unknown.

The whole white area is the next field to be explored within the map of the elliptical dialogue. This is the area of the unknown as well as the known and conscious parts of being within the relational field.

THE WHITE AREA - THE STORY OF THE ENERGETIC FIELD OF LIBIDO

Toward the end of our analytical journey Björn drew several images of a fertile nature and of himself in a different positions from the Rottweiler.

One day Björn told me:

"One has to descend to the shadow side in order to become the owner of the rock crystal."

Both in our relationship and in the frame of our elliptical analytical work, Björn made use of all the areas of the map of the elliptical dialogue. The white

Illustration Fertilized soul and soil - Photo reprinted with permission from Björn

area is the part in which Hermes was charged with psychic energy. Björn's quotations and images exemplify the energetic and constantly moving field of Hermes. In the model, I think of the white area as an area of space and possibilities; an empty yet potential area for creativity and growth that the patient can enter with the therapist. This can be both fearful and challenging. Beginning to grow from the self plane with the aid of archetypal images takes courage and will. For Björn, this development began more intensely when we had worked through his shadow complexes and lowered the tension in the mother and father complexes. When this happens, libido as psychic energy is freed, and the messenger god Hermes can serve the self of the patient in a liberated way.

Psychic energy as it is defined by Jung is called libido, or energy for life. In his essay titled *On Psychic Energy*, Jung (1912/1928 C. G. Jung CW 8) formulates his libido theory. Together with *Psychological Types* (Jung 1921 CW 6), these two texts can be read as Jung's way of systematizing the foundations of analytical psychology. Libido as psychic energy points toward movement, energy, and relationship in our psyche. This energetic field makes it possible for us as individuals and in relationship with others to catch images, fantasies, and dreams in the large fishing net of our life experiences. In analytical psychology, the concept of libido is not so much normative, but points forward and has a teleological perspective. There is also another important text to be mentioned here that is highly relevant for understanding psychic energy in the context of analytical psychology. This text was originally a paper and lecture that Jung delivered at the Tercentenary Conference of Arts and Sciences at Harvard University in September 1936 titled *Psychological Factors Determining Human Behaviour* (CW 8). At the beginning of this paper, Jung states:

> "The separation of psychology from the premises of biology is purely artificial, because the human psyche lives in indissoluble union with the body. And since these biological premises hold not only good for man, but for the whole world of living beings, the scientific basis on which they rest obtains a validity far exceeding that underlying a psychological judgement, which is valid only in the realm of consciousness."

Here Jung creates his interesting concept of instincts. He puts forward five instincts that are significant for us as human beings and therefore essential for how we as individuals express and take care of our psychic energy. These instincts are hunger, sexuality, activity, reflection, and creativity. The conference at Harvard University was titled *Factors Determining Human Behaviour*, and among the speakers were the Swiss developmental psychologist and educationalist Jean Piaget (1896-1980); the French philosopher, psychologist, and psychiatrist Pierre Janet (1859-1947); the German-American philosopher Rudolf Carnap (1891-1970); and Bronislaw Malinowski (1884-1942), the Polish-British social anthropologist who was active in the USA and at Yale University from 1938 until his death in 1942. He is famous for his anthropological science in the so-called primitive societies on the Trobiand Islands (personal notes from microfilm, CG Jung Archiv Hs 1055:751,3 ETH Zürich).

In Jung's 30-minute lecture, he emphasizes the instincts of reflection and creativity as significant for human beings. Reflection and creativity are also important for the white area on the map of the elliptical dialogue. The white area in clinical work and supervision can form a plateau from which the patient's intense memories and experiences can be explored and unpacked. This can also be an area of silence, breathing, and sitting together in the presence of the other, where emotions can be held without the need for dissociation. The white area further creates a space in which the ego-self axis can be consciously restored. In everyday life, the white area can represent the self plane, where the Jungian self is active and real. The self as centre operates in our inner and outer relationships and functions as a shared unconscious reality, where the natural world speaks to us and to the human world and its relationships.

Analytical psychology thus takes the areas of psychology, mythology, biology, and physics into account when discussing the concept of psychic energy.

We look for the elliptical and liminal realm when following the hermetic force in dialogue in the different settings of Jungian analytical work. Something is always left out, but here, in this liminal hermetic space, dialogic imaginations, images, and words can take shape with the aid of Hermes' shapes, clothes and expressions. These are the qualities ascribed to Hermes in mythology. What is left out is that which is unknown, unspoken, or not yet obvious.

HERMES AND HERMENEUTICS

Hermes is one of my favourite gods from Greek and Roman mythology. In Roman mythology and in Latin the god's name is Mercury and mercury can also relate to the heavy silvery white liquid used in thermometers. In this text I use the god's Greek name, Hermes. Hermes is a deity that possesses many qualities and is one of Zeus's many sons. Hermes's mother is Atlas's daughter Maia. He is the patron god of shepherds, travelers, orators, merchants, narrators, pickpockets, and wayfarers. From the mythological stories we learn that, already as a child, he was a successful thief. Impressed by his skills, Zeus equipped him with a winged helmet and winged sandals, which can still be seen today in emblems and advertisements. Hermes is also messenger for the gods between the infernal region of Hades and the human world and a guide of souls.

In *The Odyssey* (Homer 1946/1991), the gods send Hermes to tell Odysseus that the time has come for him to leave his cave of pleasure on the Island of Calypsos. Although he longs for home, he has not been able to begin this part of his individuation journey. But now there is no return, and his quiet life of pleasure and lamentation for home are over.

> "Zeus now turned to Hermes his beloved son. 'Hermes,' he said, 'as you are our usual Messenger, convey our final decision to that Nymph of the plaited tresses. The long enduring Odysseus must now set out for home. On the journey he shall have neither gods nor men to help him." (Odyssey 5:26-31. p 71)

Hermes takes messages to Odysseus and makes plans for his individuation journey.

In late ancient history, Hermes Trismegistos, the threefold great Hermes, was worshipped and considered to be the author of Corpus Hermeticum. During the Renaissance, these scriptures were considered to contain great wisdom. The adjective hermetical, as in hermetically sealed, also stems from Hermes. In Norway, all kinds of tinned food or goods are called *hermetikk*. The Mercurius staff, the attribute of Hermes, is called Caduceus in Latin and is known as the staff of the two snakes. Hermes used the staff as an attribute of Psykopompos, the guide of souls. The staff was given to him by Apollo in exchange for a lyre. Hermes invented and created the lyre himself on his first day of life. As a newborn, he crawled from his cradle, killed a tortoise, put strings on her shell, returned to the cradle, and began to play the lyre with all his might.

In the field of Jungian psychoanalysis, Hermes is often used as a symbol of movement and change. In Jung's autobiography (C. G. Jung 1961/1989), he describes a dream that he had around Christmastime in 1912, after parting with Freud. This dream became the starting point for his confrontation with the unconscious. He had reached a dead end in his conscious dialogue with himself on the question, "What myth does man live nowadays?" and "Do you live in it?" His answer was no. "But then what is your myth—the myth in which you live?"

"...In the dream I found myself in a magnificent Italian loggia with pillars... I was sitting on a gold Renaissance chair; in front of me was a table of great beauty. It was made of green stone, like emerald....Suddenly a white bird descended...Immediately, the dove was transformed into a little girl...Then she suddenly vanished; the dove was back and spoke slowly in human voice. "Only in the first hours of the night can I transform myself into a human being, while the male dove is busy with the twelve dead." Then she flew off into the blue air, and I awoke."

Jung's reflections on his dream are as follows:

"I was greatly stirred. What business would a male dove be having with twelve dead people? In connection with the emerald table the story of the Tabula Smaragdina occurred to me, the emerald table in the alchemical legend of Hermes Trismegistos. He was said to have left behind him a table upon which the basic tenets of alchemical wisdom were engraved in Greek."

From the beginning of analytical psychology Jung interpreted dreams and symbols in order to help his patients understand themselves. In his own life, this dream signifies the entrance of the alchemical legend of Hermes Trismegistos.

In his book *Hermes Guide of Souls* (1976, 2003), C. G. Jung's friend Karl Kerényi (1897- 1973) presents a lively portrait of Hermes. Károly Kerényi was a Hungarian scholar of classical philology and one of the founders of modern studies of Greek mythology. In his book, he provides us with the archetypal background for the guiding of souls and at the same time connects his text to the guiding of souls into psychotherapy. He blends together the meaning of the god Hermes with analytical psychology in an excellent way.

Hermeneutics (from the Greek *hermeneutike*, *techne*, art of interpretation *hermneu'o*) is a theological and philosophical discipline that can help us to see that which is difficult to understand. Augustinos (354-430), one of the most important church fathers in the West, worked out an *ars interpretandi* — the art of text interpretation. Friedrich Schleiermacher (1768-1834), a German theologian and philosopher, worked in the same tradition and wrote about philosophical reflections on interpretation. His hermeneutics was concerned with seeing and widening the subjective experience of interpretation with a view to improving and deepening understanding. In connection with his thoughts, today we use the terms *double circular and spiral train of thoughts and movements* when interpreting texts. Schleiermacher, through his understanding of hermeneutics, thus made an important contribution to the history of philosophy. He lifted hermeneutics from the art of interpretation in a theological context to a general form of art related to understanding. His thoughts in this area inspired the further development of hermeneutic theory by German philosopher Hans-Georg Gadamer (1900-2002). Gadamer was deeply rooted in the hermeneutic tradition (branch) of scholarship and developed new perspectives on health and illness in conjunction with human dialogue. He maintained that meaning was born in and through language, in the dialogue itself, rather than within individuals' own senses.

How might a healthy balance in life be described? We have all experienced different events and happenings in childhood. Do you remember when your parents explained that when you were ill, you had to stay at home and in bed? Later in life you probably became more familiar with this and experienced a loss of balance when illness struck. What is remarkable is that balance is not so much connected to the actual illness but to the experience of being healthy, when you feel balanced and at the same time in tune with the rhythm of life, your body, your relationships, and your inner image of yourself. Feeling healthy in the sense of an experience of wholeness in life cannot be measured in terms of standards. It is rather an inner state of balance that emerges from a coordinated state of being.

The function of pain in our bodies and souls leads to subjective awareness of feelings and sensitivities which tells us that it is a disturbance present in the balance and equilibrium of our ongoing life processes. When the pain becomes too much to bear and we want to do something about it, or we long for another state of being, we will probably consult a doctor or psychotherapist, or even look for a Jungian psychoanalyst. It is at this point of disturbed balance that we can catch a sight of and understand what kind of energies exist and create balance and health in our life systems (Gadamer 2003). We undergo treatment, perhaps as a Jungian psychoanalytical journey of individuation. But what does it mean to "treat" someone? This use of language also points beyond the analytical relationship. We treat each other without necessarily being analysts, doctors, psychotherapists, or psychologists. We treat each other well, and sometimes badly. But what are we "doing" then? The task is perhaps to treat someone in the "right" way. Does that mean that we follow rules? I would prefer to say we treat someone well by talking to them in a way that does not make them think or behave as I want them to. Treating someone well means recognizing and confirming the other person in the quality of being the Other. It is not about prescriptions or measurements. It is only when we serve as a guide for others and recognize their quality of being that they are able to find their own differentiated, special way. As Jung writes in the *The Red Book* (2009 p. 231), "The way is within us…" Only under these conditions can we be guides and companions for others in order for them to find their own special, separate, individual ways. Treatment should therefore always include and embrace liberation and be aimed at setting the other free. This requires a certain responsibility but also in a liberating way, providing and caring for the other.

Every treatment serves nature. From Greek, we have the word therapy (origin Greek *therapeia* 'healing'). Every treatment also includes being foreseeable (foresight, foreseeing) and considerate to the other. Trust, relationship, dialogue, and mutuality are the basic conditions for therapy when we embark on a mutual journey toward health and balance. Dialogue is the most important tool in treatment, because it is a determining factor for the experience of being understood and listened to. The perspective of keeping and holding balance is necessary in the elliptical dialogue but is not always easy. We are all aware of the difficulties in understanding each other in relationships. Dealing with unequal relationships is also one of the most difficult tasks in the human act of being together. Regardless of whether we are fathers and sons, mothers and daughters, husbands and wives, teachers, psychoanalysts, doctors, all the professionals with some kind of relationship to students, clients, patients and customers—we all have difficulty understanding each other. There is always the risk of doing too much in our eagerness to help and understand, so that balance is lost. When discussing the risk of doing too much, Gadamer (2003) quotes Rilke from *Duinoelegies*: "...wo sich das reine Zuwenig unbegreiflich verwandelt -, umspringt in jenes leere Zuviel." "...the unspeakable space appears where purity of insufficiency transforms into overly efficient emptiness" (Rilke fifth Duinoelegy). I think that this is a good description of how balance and equilibrium get lost in an exaggerated effort to be helpful. It leads us toward health as the rhythm of life, an uninterrupted course of events where balance is present, not as a static steady state but as a state of movement. The three basic phenomena that are present and form the ground conditions for life are breathing, metabolization, and sleep. They create the necessary conditions for living, rebuilding energy, and recovery.

One of Jung's most important contributions to depth psychology is his perspective of the individual psyche. Jung's fundamental question is: What is a human being meant to be from the innermost ground of being? The concern is about the conditions necessary for health and balance. Analytical psychology is thus rooted in biology, philosophy, and physics. From a contemporary psychological perspective, Jung's ideas correspond well with Aaron Antonovsky's (1923-1994) concepts of salutogenes and sense of coherence (SOC, in Swedish KASAM) and with the ideas of life cycle psychologists like Erik H. Erikson (1902-1994).

Principium individuationis is a concept used by Jung in *Septem Sermones ad Mortuos* in January 1916. The phrase has a long history from philosophy and is brought to presence in analytical psychology. In his later writings, in 1921, Jung defines individuation as follows:

"The concept of individuation plays a large role in our psychology. In general, it is a process by which individual beings are formed and differentiated;

in particular, it is the development of the psychological **individual** (q.v.) as a being distinct from a general, collective psychology. Individuation, therefore, is a process of **differentiation** (q.v.), having for its goal the development of the individual personality." (Psychological Types CW 6 §757.)

Individuation points toward movement and creativity in a life and can be seen at work in the energetic field of libido. The movements is both toward separation and differentiation and as a development from unconscious layers to wholeness comes a consciousness of purpose and a synthesising movement.

At the end of his book Kerényi (1976/2003) refers to the slender elegance of the dynamic pair of Hermes and Silenos as the figures on a Berlin vase (Buschor 1940) from the early classical period of 500-490 B.C. The delicate figure of a deer between them hints at the untamed world, and they all stand on a surface etched with the hermeneutical lines of eternal rhythm and spirals. Like Odysseus when he sets out for Ithaka, it is not possible to shy away from the dangers of the most profound depths or be unaffected by the new pathways that Hermes is always prepared to open.

Hermeneutical movements in the individuation journey form the overarching idea and the underground preparations necessary for the elliptical dialogue to flow in the whole white area.

GREGORY BATESON ENCOUNTERS JUNG'S *SEPTEM SERMONES AD MORTUOS*

How does the elliptical dialogue fit into the borderlands of C. G. Jung's and Gregory Bateson's analytical psychology and systems theory? When I studied systems theory and family therapy in the 1980s, Bateson was important due to his approach to relationships in families and also to larger systems like organizations and communities. Systems theory is then relevant for relationships from the personal to the collective level.

Bateson was born in England in 1904 and died in California in 1980, which meant that he was a generation younger than Jung. He came from an academic family, and his father, William Bateson, a famous biologist, was the world's first professor of genetics. Gregory Bateson had an interdisciplinary approach, and as an anthropologist he was interested in how living things were connected. For example, he studied Bali culture with his first wife, Margaret Mead, communication in families when living in California, how dolphins interacted, and how thinking was done (epistemology).

C.G. Jung's Septem Sermones Ad Mortuos
by Gregory Bateson

This tiny book is for me the greatest achievement of Jung's life – the turning point in a long battle. He clearly recognizes in Memories, Dreams, Reflections that the days (in 1916) in which it was written were the beginning of all his later insights.

At that time he was coming out of a long period of slow recovery from the influence of Freud and from the break with Freud. It was the moment for a new for return to a very old) natural history of Man-God-Cosmos.

The book is difficult to read. It is (of course) a sort of poetry, and therefore almost impossible to be reviewed and analysed in prose. And Jung's views clearly changed as he wrote, even in the three or four days of the writing. He was in a state of *transition.*

Man is a gateway, through which from the outer world of gods, daemons, and souls ye [the Dead] shall pass into the inner world, out of the greater into the smaller world. Small and transitory is man ... At immeasurable distance standeth one single Star in the zenith.

The book then both *is* a progress from macrocosm to microcosm and is a description of the landscape at various stages of that progress.

It is not clear (does not matter) who is the novice and who the initiator in this strange catechism. Not only Jung but also the Dead are in transition. They came "back from Jerusalem, where they found not what they sought."

Excerpt from Jung's Septem Sermones ad Mortuos (Seven Sermons to the Dead) →

SERMO I

THE dead came back from Jerusalem, where they found not what they sought. They prayed me let them in and besought my word, and thus I began my teaching.

Harken: I begin with nothingness. Nothingness is the same as fullness. In infinity full is no better than empty. Nothingness is both empty and full. As well might ye say anything else of nothingness, as for instance, white is it, or black, or again, it is not, or it is. A thing that is infinite and eternal hath no qualities, since it hath all qualities.

This nothingness or fullness we name the PLEROMA. Therein both thinking and being cease, since the eternal and infinite possess no qualities. In it no being is, for he then would be distinct from the pleroma, and would possess qualities which would distinguish him as something distinct from the pleroma.

In the pleroma there is nothing and everything. is quite fruitless to think about the pleroma, for t would mean self-dissolution.

CREATURA is not in the pleroma, but in its The pleroma is both beginning and end of crea beings. It pervadeth them, as the light of the s

From his state of transition, Jung sees three concepts to which he gives the Gnostic names: Pleroma, Creatura and Abraxas. There is also – man.

Abraxas is approximately, Shiva, the ultimate Creator-Destroyer. The most terrible and most beautiful of all the gods that man contains within his macrocosmic self and that in turn is contained in the macrocosm. Within Abraxas, the more familiar figures (Helios, the Sun; and the Devil, darkness) are subsumed. But it is Abraxas that gets the poetry.

It is splendid as a lion in the instant he striketh down his victim.

It is beautiful as a day in Spring.

To look upon it, is blindness.

To know it, is sickness.

To worship it, is death.

To fear it, is wisdom.

To resist it not, is redemption.

Gregory Bateson and review from The Next Whole Earth Catalog (1974/1980.) Figure Created by Gunilla Midbøe

Bateson believed that we live in a world that is only made up of relationships. "Patterns that connect" is a key metaphor in Bateson's work. In one of his lectures, he says: "You have probably thought that you have five fingers. (…) What is important is not five but four relations between the fingers" (N. Bateson, 2011).

For me, something was lacking in this systemic approach. This was the individual concept of the unknown, the unconscious, and the territory of dreams, symbols, and myths. As you might imagine, I was thrilled to discover that the link between Bateson and Jung was *Septem Sermones ad Mortuos*, or *Seven Sermons to The Dead*. This was a turning point both in my professional development and in my personal life.

Septem Sermones ad Mortuos was introduced to Bateson by Jungian analyst Jane Wheelwright in the 1960s. Bateson read the text and later reported that he was profoundly influenced by it.

Jung wrote *Septem Sermones* in January and February of 1916. He was then 40 years of age and felt compelled from within to formulate and express what his inner teacher, Philemon, might have said. This explains why this peculiar language came into being. The Dead came back from Jerusalem unable to find what they were looking for. They were the voices of the Unanswered, Unresolved, and Unredeemed. We can think of them as unindividuated souls coming back to the living world for transformation in order to fulfill their individuation journey so that they can finally find peace. We can read this text again in *Scrutinies*, in *The Red Book*, where the dialogue between Jung's "I" and Philemon gives it an extra dimension.

Bateson's response to the text was both **aesthetic and theoretical** and formed the starting point for his Theory of Mind.

In the review (S. Brand, ed., 1974, 1980) he wrote, I quote:

"C. G. Jung's

SEPTEM SERMONES AD MORTUOS
by Gregory Bateson

This tiny book is for me the greatest achievement of Jung's life – the turning point in a long battle. He clearly recognises in Memories, Dreams, Reflections that the days (in 1916) in which it was written were the beginning of all his later insights.

At that time he was coming out of a long period of slow recovery from the influence of Freud and from the break with Freud. It was the moment for a new (or return to a very old) natural history of Man-God-Cosmos.

The book is difficult to read. **It is (of course) a sort of poetry and therefore almost impossible to be reviewed and analysed in prose. And Jung's views clearly changed as he wrote, even in the three or four days of the writing. He was in a state of *transition*.**

Man is a gateway, through which from the outer world of gods, daemons, and souls ye (the Dead) shall pass into the inner world; out of the greater into the smaller world. Small and transitory is man... At immeasurable distance standeth one single Star at the zenith.

The book then both is a progress from macrocosm to microcosm and is a description of the landscape at various stages at that progress.

It is not clear (does not matter) who is the novice and who the initiator in this strange catechism. **Not only Jung but also**

the Dead are in transition. They came "back from Jerusalem, where they found not what they sought."

From his state of transition, Jung sees three concepts to which he gives the Gnostic names: Pleroma, Creatura and Abraxas. There is also – man.

Abraxas is approximately Shiva, the ultimate Creator – Destroyer. The most terrible and most beautiful of all the gods that man contains within his microcosmic self and that in turn is contained in the macrocosm. Within Abraxas, the more familiar figures (Helios, the Sun; and the Devil, darkness) are subsumed. But it is Abraxas that gets the poetry.

> *It is splendid as a lion in the instant he*
> *striketh down his victim*
> *It is beautiful as a day in Spring.*
> *To look upon it, is blindness.*
> *To know it, is sickness.*
> *To worship it, is death.*
> *To fear it, is wisdom.*
> *To resist it not, is redemption.*

All this is within creatura, the realm where differences, distinctions, and ideas hold sway. The ground out of which creatura looms as figure (in the language of Gestalt theory) is pleroma —the totally unconceived and unstructured realm about which nothing can be said or thought because to say anything is to create distinction. Call it "void" or "fullness," it is still older and deeper than that first distinction by which creatura comes into recognition and therefore being.

The book is exasperating, profound and beautiful."

The following are the main points and indicate how Bateson used the text in his Theory of Mind, as he presents it in *Mind and Nature* (2002) and in *Angels Fear Towards an Epistemology of the Sacred* (2005):

• **The pattern that connects is a metapattern.** He connected **epistemology** (how thinking is done, how we know what we know) and **ontology** (our nature of being), which resulted in a starting point for his theory of mind. **The starting point is in the *interface* between**

Pleroma, the crude domain governed only by forces and impacts and Creatura, a domain governed by distinctions and differences. This allowed him to step out of the Cartesian dichotomy, from either-or to both-and.

- **The map is not the territory.** The interface between Creatura and Pleroma becomes a pathway and a bridge for messages.

- **A difference that makes a difference is a difference over time and is change.** In Jungian analytical understanding, this condition is needed for principium individuationis, the process of individuation.

- Relationship is always a product of double description, and this **double view *is* the relationship**. Think of Bateson's hand metaphor.

Both Jung and, toward the end of his life, Bateson, created maps of knowledge that in my view can give meaning to our theoretical and clinical concepts of today. They both did that out of the profound archetypal poetic rhythm of *Septem Sermones ad Mortuos*.

At the end of Bateson's life, he worked with his daughter Mary Catherine on *Angels Fear* (Bateson & Bateson, 1987). In this work, Bateson highlights the interface between *Creatura* and *Pleroma*. Jung insisted on the contrast between the domain of Pleroma, which is a *massa confusa* or *prima materia* governed by a cosmic soup of forces, and Creatura, the domain governed by distinctions and differences. This is also the domain where principium individuationis comes into being. It is in this liminal border space between Creatura and Pleroma that Hermes and hermeneutic energy are active. For Gregory Bateson, it became clear that there could be no maps in Pleroma, only in Creatura. Whatever gets from territory to map is for him *news of difference* and therefore a synonym for information. His focus in this liminal space was on what he called "syllogisms in metaphor." According to the Oxford Dictionary, a syllogism is a form of reasoning in which a conclusion is drawn from two propositions (e.g., all dogs are animals; all animals have four legs; therefore, all dogs have four legs). In this space, with the aid of Jung's *Septem Sermones ad Mortuos*, he was able to tie together his lifelong interest of sublingual communication that is common in myth, playfulness, madness, animal communication, and art. He was interested in forming a creatural grammar based on what he called "syllogisms in metaphor," i.e., the patterns and communication of language using similes and metaphors in a variety of embedded and embodied ways.

What does this mean in practical terms? For Bateson, the Pleroma has no mental process, no name, and no class. The Creatura, on the other hand, is based on pattern and communicates through language using similes and metaphors. In language, classical logic builds on causal word structures called syllogisms that follow the pattern, "if this is true, than that is true." In other words, if Socrates is a man, and if all men die, then Socrates will die. But there is another word structure that Bateson describes as built on likeness, for example: "Grass dies, men die (therefore) men are grass." Logicians disapprove of this kind of syllogism because it does not make sense (they call it "affirming the consequent"), but Bateson believed that this formula indicated the way in which the natural world communicated. He formulated this credo:

> …"the process of making a metaphor has some wider significance—(it) may indeed be a basic characteristic of Creatura. …It becomes evident that metaphor is not just pretty poetry, it is not either good or bad logic, but is in fact the logic upon which the biological world has been built, the main characteristic and organizing glue of this world of mental processes that I have been trying to sketch for you." (Bateson & Bateson, 1987/2005, pp. 26-30).

Jung's text, which Bateson received from Jungian analyst Jane Wheelwright, served as a Hermes force and enabled him to connect his theory with spirituality. It was the igniting spark. Jung helped Bateson to find a view of the mind and the universe that was neither mechanistic nor supernatural. It was the identity of the physical and the psychic world to unite mind and matter, like the title of Bateson's work *Mind and Nature – A Necessary Unity* (1979/2002). Here it is also relevant to think of Jung's profound studies in alchemy and about the concept of *unus mundus*. In CW 14 § 766, Jung writes:

> "With this conjecture of the identity of the psychic and the physical we approach the alchemical view of the **unus mundus**, the potential world of the first day of creation, when there was as yet 'no second'…for all the alchemists matter had a divine aspect, whether on the ground that God was imprisoned in it in the form of the **anima mundi** or **anima media natura**, or that matter represented God's 'reality.'"

Bateson also experienced *Septem Sermones ad Mortuos* as what he called a metalogue. This is an interesting and creative concept that fits well with the elliptical dialogue and hermeneutical movements of monologue, dialogue, trialogue, and metalogue. Bateson's definition of metalogue is that it is a conversation about some aspect of mental process in which ideally the interaction exemplifies the subject matter. This is exactly what he felt when reading *Septem Sermones ad Mortuos* and what he describes in the above review. To me, this corresponds with Jung's concept of the transcendent function and of his psychology of the transference (C. G. Jung CW 8 pp. 67-91 and CW 16 pp. 163-323). In this energetic mental process of interaction that Bateson refer to, the metalogue he experienced when assimilating *Septem Sermones ad Mortuos* and his own understanding of cybernetics, he was creatively helped to synthesise his theory of mind and nature. Batesons reading and assimilation from two perspectives (one from the perspective of physics and cybernetics and the other from the spiritual and mind perspective) lead forward to a formulation of this theory of mind and nature and how the interconnectedness of mind and matter could be understood. So now the white area of the elliptical dialogue is inhabited by the energetic field of libido, hermeneutics, and, finally, cybernetics.

CYBERNETICS

Cybernetics is the science of communications and automatic control systems in machines and living things, and originates from the Greek *kuberne˜te˜s* "steersman." Bateson was a part of the cybernetic group that met at the Macy Conferences from 1946-1953 and was funded by the Josiah Macy Jr. Foundation. The interdisciplinary nature of the group attracted Bateson, as well as the mathematician Norbert Wiener, the neurophysiologist Warren McCulloch, the German psychologist Kurt Lewin, the English ecologist G. Evelyn Hutchinson (a one-time school friend of Bateson), and the German engineer Heinz Von Foerster. From these beginnings cybernetics has developed to embrace a whole range of ideas about information flow and control within systems, particularly in circular and more complex systems. Bateson was attracted by its interdisciplinary nature. Having initially studied biology, he was able to use many of his biological insights in the anthropological research he conducted with Margaret Mead, which in turn led to new psychological ideas in social and clinical psychology. The theories produced during these years include the "double-bind theory" and the understanding of "hierarchies" in communication. However, the central concept that Gregory Bateson developed was the understanding that all the systems in the living world have a mind, in the sense that every system is interrelated and nested within larger mental systems to the extent that they form an ultimate interconnected whole, which for Jung was "the sacred" Anima Mundi.

The understanding and position in the system of the analyst and supervisor is important for understanding the cybernetics in the elliptical dialogue. In first-order cybernetics, the therapist's role includes giving advice, writing prescriptions, or making interpretations—rather like a coach or behavioural therapist in an orthodox sense, where behavioural analyses and manuals are working tools. In second-order cybernetics, within psychotherapy and psychoanalysis, one takes part in and allows oneself to be transformed in a deep sense. In fact, in this position, it is also possible to be a teller, a listener, or a reflective person, providing that some kind of context is provided that is accepted by the system as a whole, i.e., in analysis, supervision, or a lecture. Language plays a crucial role here, because language helps us to move into a pool of force where we are affected and moved by Hermes in the guise in which he appears. He may appear as destructive, constructive, cheating, or just running around, creating chaos. I can imagine Hermes's energy both in analytical settings with one person or with a couple or family. Also, when supervising in group settings, this hermeneutical imagination can, when it is allowed to make itself clear and become observable, provide me with inner images that can help to keep a group contained and in balance. It is a kind of inner active imagination in the actual context that energizes my self-field and allows symbolic and archetypal images to rise within me. It helps me to stay connected to my ego-self axis and allow me freedom of bodily and verbal movement.

In my opinion, the position of the analyst is important for reflection and awareness of the standpoint. Questions such as "Am I a listening participant" or "Am I a talking and reflective participant" are important to ask. Knowing what kind of system one is a participant in is also vital: Is it a system of myself and a family, a system of myself and an analysand, or a system of myself and a group?

I became more acquainted with second-order cybernetics when studying epistemology as a ground model as understood by Bateson from a cybernetic perspective and by second-wave cyberneticists such as Humberto Maturana, Franscisco Varela, Heinz von Foerster, and Ernst von Glasersfeld. Humberto Maturana, along with Franscisco Varela, was a biologist from the beginning but with a strong philosophical orientation. They are particularly known for creating the term autopoesis about the nature of reflexive feedback mechanisms in living systems and concepts such as structural determinism and structure coupling. In their work, they were interested in how the system as structure reacted. This was an idea that from the beginning influenced the family therapy setting as well. The result, on one hand, could be that it gave a too static picture of human systems without considering the individual's unconscious layers. This was one of my own arguments for turning to analytical psychology.

Jung also started to form his theory in the beginning of 1900, when physics was a developing science and psychology was in its beginning. In the struggle to integrate physics with psychology and not only transport concepts into understanding of human psyche, he turned to alchemy. From alchemical studies, he formed an epistemological ground on how to understand the transformation of mind and matter. In alchemy, content and process are not divided but are reciprocal aspects of human communication. This forms and transforms toward wholeness and individuation within a person in using language for dialogues, listening, and reflecting. This also forms and transforms the analyst into a participant of the analytical system where my own language, when in the analyst position, is the result of present dialogues and personal and professional history. Analysis and supervision become a "withness."

When reflecting on alchemy and second-order cybernetics and even an eco-systemic perspective (Auerswald, Fam Proc 26: 317 – 330, 1987), their epistemologies can be seen as coexisting and can bring together both Bateson's development and Jung's development. In Alchemical Studies Jung is very contemporary and up to date about this when he reflects on Chinese philosophy as he is writing a foreword to *The Secret of the Golden Flower* (1931/1962, trans. Richard Wilhelm) titled *Modern Psychology Offers a Possibility of Understanding*:

> "Now and then it happened in my practice that a patient grew beyond himself because of unknown potentialities, and this became an experience of prime importance to me. In the meantime I had learned that all the greatest and most important problems of life are fundamentally insoluble. They must be so, for they express the necessary polarity inherent in every self-regulating system. They can never be solved, but only outgrown."
> (C.G. Jung 1968/1981 CW 13, § 18)

A clinical experience in analytical work with Helen of this transformation can be found in Part II, *The impossible question or the missing bone/leg*.

It is important to be clear about the conditions for entering into the elliptical dialogue and to keep in mind that this entrance includes the whole white energetic area of flowing energies. This is a tentative work, as well as a work for exploration and clarification. Dialogue in its different forms has to be an option. This is clarified by container questions and exploring areas of context, contract, and contact for the possible analytical work to come. For example, in couples' psychotherapy as well as in individual analytical work, the expectation can be that everything will be fine if the other person changes. Unpacking an attitude like this and becoming more aware of communication patterns are important. It is also about clarifying the difference between changing and transforming. In psychoanalytical language, it is about withdrawing projections and transforming out of increased consciousness more than out of prescriptive will decision. In Jungian terms, it is to do with catching sight of our shadow and our shadow projections on the other. There is nothing strange or pathological about these interactive relationship patterns. Whether they are for good or ill can be explored by letting the spotlight shine on the interactive pattern in order to clarify and outline its contours. Pointing out to a couple that they have an exceptional position for transforming and can work on their relationship and experiment with different positions can be a great relief—as well as a huge challenge. I see the different conditions for entering into the elliptical dialogue as context markers that can be recaptured in different time intervals.

PART I
THE ELLIPTICAL DIALOGUE

2. The elliptical dialogue as a map for Jungian supervision

Supervision in psychotherapy and different forms of psychosocial work can take place in a number of frameworks. I have been a member of supervision groups and have been individually supervised. I also find myself in the role of a supervisor in professional teams and individual settings. This work is mostly ongoing in public health care, psychiatry, and the social health and welfare system in Sweden. My Jungian psychoanalytical background helps me to focus on the symbolic function and the ego-self relation in the supervision setting. The map of the elliptical dialogue is also a useful tool in this setting.

The Swedish word for supervision is *handledning*, which literary translated means taking someone by the hand and leading them. The Swedish word handled means wrist and thus points to the area between the hand and the arm. Together with the English term supervision, which to me suggests a meta-perspective on a case or relationship, these two terms can create the gateway from which to enter the elliptical dialogue in a supervision setting. The elliptical dialogue is a collaborative work that is performed and transformed within the space and arena of the blue frame. Here, the blue frame refers to the definition of the given and accepted assignment. This is about being as clear as possible for the container questions of context, contract, and contact. It is good to invite the person with organizational responsibility for the team to the first supervision meeting. I then initiate a dialogue with the officer in charge of the team in the presence of the team members and the professionals who are going to be part of the supervisory group. This is, of course, done with the agreement of the participants. The overall aim is to formulate the aims and objectives of the supervision and to introduce myself and how I see supervision. This initial dialogue with the officer in charge can help to clarify issues such as how the officer in charge defines the group's strengths and possible areas for development, the kind of hierarchy that exists in the organization, what the officer in charge thinks about informal power structures, and what happens when different members of the group start to criticize the management. This is an expression of professional individuation and transformation both as a team and as individuals. These are important areas for reflection and clarification. Supervision in groups as well as in individual settings makes a space for the shadow dynamics to emerge and to foresee this development by putting it into dialogue in the blue frame as a natural part of supervision dynamics and can lower tensions within the organization. The shadow aspects can then be seen as part of growth in the professional individuation. Here, the blue frame can help to formulate the kinds of limits and restrictions that are necessary in the organization. It also puts the question of loyalty on the table and defines the formal limits of the organization and whether there is room for team members to maneuver between the different hierarchical levels if this becomes necessary. The blue frame can also help to introduce reflective discussions within the institution or working unit. It is also important to discuss how the cooperation between the different team members will be managed.

In the reflective work involved in the supervision, it is important to assess what happens at the different levels and structures of the elliptical dialogue and to listen carefully to members of the team. In this context, staying within the different team members' expressions—and only their expressions—is imperative. Preoccupation with people's expressions is important in supervision, analytical work, and family therapy work. When meeting a group of professionals or the person being supervised, being able to listen to their outer and inner body language is vital.

But what does "staying within the different team members' expressions" mean? When we are concerned with words in an analytical setting, we need to see a person's reactions to their own expressions. They might lean forward, smile, cry, or jiggle a foot up and down. The point is to capture what it is they said that led to the reaction. The point is also to tolerate our own bodily reactions so that we allow a silence to unfold, allow the crying to take place, and calmly stay in the moment and be concerned about why they reacted in the way they did to what they said. We can then get hold of what they said, repeat it from our own position as analysts and/or supervisors, and then help them to talk about it. For example, when I asked Björn what he saw in the word **"fearful,"** or when someone is thoughtful or tense in the context of supervision, it is possible to find out what led to the reaction. This leads to an assimilation of expressions we can begin to unpack and look at not what lies behind or under them, but what is in the expression itself. In this sense I like to be watchful and attentive to words that indicate growth and germination. If the germinating seed is exposed to too much sunlight too quickly, it loses its elasticity and becomes limp. The same happens if it is given too much water. These kinds of words need to be part of a language that is contained in an emotional context. The map of the elliptical dialogue can thus provide a helpful structure, like an espalier, trellis, or lattice that supports the birth of coherent narratives in the life of the analysand, in the analytical work being done, and in the supervisory work at hand in the individual or group setting.

Similarly, in *Philosophical Investigations* (p. 262), Wittgenstein talks about the inponderable evidence that belongs to the delicate shades and nuances of the gaze, gesture, and tones:

"The utmost shades of meaning belong to the unweightable finest nuances of the gaze, the gesture and the tone."

GUIDELINES FOR SUPERVISION DIALOGUES

In the following, I provide areas or fields for exploration that I find especially useful when working within supervision. I have found these guidelines helpful because they indicate the organic nature of the supervisory process. They are not intended as a manual or set of rules to follow. The intention is to allow a new language and new imaginations to emerge from the dialogue and enrich the clinical psychotherapeutic work being undertaken.

What I want to convey in supervision involves approaches to the other. The idea of "not-knowing" can be a way of addressing the unconscious. I strive to provide a space for dialogue and a process for being able to be in relationship and conversation with each other. From this, new meaning is generated through the words and the stories and new perspectives for learning and experience created. This applies both in relation to colleagues in the working group and in relation to patients and their families and contexts.

In analytical psychology the concept of individuation is central to psychological development. What do we see when we look into the word individuation? In this part, the concept of individuation is explored from the perspective of the individual as a professional psychotherapist. I see this as a highly personal individuation journey in relation to my own life and professional experiences. The professional individuation journey is intimately linked to our personal life. For Jung, the formulation of his theory and practice of analytical psychology went hand in hand with the inner exploration of his unconscious and his own experiences of dreams and inner images. In *The Red Book* (Jung 2009), we can see the deep layers of Jung's individuation journey and the experiences that are linked to the theoretical and methodological concepts of analytical psychology. Jung never became locked into one philosophical system. This might make him perhaps difficult to read if we expect a linear link to his method from philosophers. However, there is a link from the ancient Gnostic thinkers and medieval alchemists to early thinkers such as Goethe, Kant, Schopenhauer, Carus, Hartmann, and Nietzsche (Stein 1998/2006 p. 5). The bottom line of Jung's understanding of the human psyche is a deep experience of the mystery of human existence and an ongoing struggle with questions that cannot be put into boxes of fixed systems.

In addition to the individuation process, Jung developed two other methods for observing and developing the human psyche that I find highly relevant for professional individuation. Like craftsmen and artists, we too have tools and instruments that we can use in our work as psychoanalysts and supervisors. These tools are uniquely and individually forged by experience of life and professional training. Like the medieval alchemists in their workshops, we equip our interior and exterior workshops with suitable tools. But the alchemists were also in tune with the deep mystery of the human soul and prepared themselves to be open to the mercurial energy of the psyche. In their world, they let the energized power of Hermes work. For us as contemporary professionals in our different settings, I think that this orientation and attitude is worth highlighting. In practice, it can take the form of meditating and tuning in to the tasks and meetings that lie ahead before a professional session with individuals, couples, a family, or supervision, and tuning in to the inner psychic world after each professional session in order to become more aware of the images and fantasies that my own unconscious came up with as a professional craftsman. In analytical psychology, the method of *amplification* is useful for giving space to and formulating in words what comes to mind in accordance with a specific symbol or fantasy from the unconscious. Jung used this technique to see what the symbol could be compared within cultures, religions, and myths—not as a free associative runaway loop in any direction, but as a movement that is consistent with the symbol given by the unconscious. We can think of this movement as a tree, with its trunk as a backbone and the different branches stretched out to the world to catch the surrounding living creatures in the air, but all the time anchored by its roots in the earth. Jung also developed the technique of active imagination as a way of entering the inner world of dreams more deeply. Experienced psychoanalysts and supervisors can also benefit from this, especially if there is a deep respect for integrity and the preservation of the psyche. In the clinical part two of this book, I elaborate on this idea in the context of the analytical work undertaken with Björn and how my own active imagination became a way of finding an emergent third area in our relationship. This third area then became the dynamic field of the self that was activated in us both.

In the context of what I call Jungian supervision, I introduce four steps with questions that I have found helpful when sorting, understanding, and opening up to new perspectives on reflective processes in supervision and clinical work. They are meant as suggestions in order to capture the underlying network of language and dialogues that bind people together rather than as structuring issues in an operational method. Two main movements are involved: the differentiating or separating movement; and the synthesising, coagulating movement toward the "third" area, i.e., where one plus one equals three and where "not-knowing" means moving toward the transcendence of knowledge about the third "image."

In order to make room for our own and our clients' polyphony of voices (internal and external), this approach needs to respect privacy and emerge from the interaction of, and collaboration with, different reality perspectives.

Step 1: Context for the case.

- What kind of dialogues within yourself or with others made you want to present the case right now?

- What do you want to achieve by presenting the case, and how can we or I contribute to your wish?

These questions help to focus on the relationship between the supervisor and the therapist and on the therapist's relationship and expectations of help and feedback from colleagues on the team. They are meant as openings— for creating space and making room for ideas and imaginations of different realities in the context of the supervisory session and opening up the reflective movement in which Hermes can begin to make himself present. This step can be seen as an energetic charging of the white area on the map of the elliptical dialogue.

Step 2: Mapping the referral process.

- How did you get involved in this case?

- Whom have you been in dialogue with and why?

If the case has been referred by another care professional or if other helpers are involved:

- How might the expectations of others affect the results of the treatment? Are these expectations similar to yours or different?

- What did you think about the case before the first session, and have your thoughts changed during the analytical process?

The above questions focus on the referral process and introduce the contexts of all those involved.

Step 3: The client's and family members' images.

- How do the client/family members express themselves about their difficulties? How do they define the problem, and what do they say and tell you about it?

- How do they think the treatment should proceed, and do they see any solution of the painful situation that made them apply/be recommended for psychotherapy?

This area explores different ideas about the situation and how the problems might be solved. A central point here is that ideas can both compete with and contribute to getting stuck in the creative process of treatment.

Step 4: The "third" synthesising image.

- What are your expectations so far of what might be achieved in the case, and how do these expectations reflect those of the other people involved? What is realistic, and what is unrealistic?

- What have others tried to do, and what was the outcome?

This puts the focus on the judgment of the ego-self axis both within the system and also among the different individuals in the system. What could be achieved? It also helps to determine whether the therapist or other helpers are continuing to try out the suggested solutions independent of reflective feedback from others.

THE ELLIPTICAL DIALOGUE IN GROUP SUPERVISION

When a word is spoken, it passes from a speaker to a receiving listener. The word has meaning for both of them, but does it have the same meaning for them both? We need to consider the possibility that meanings differ.

Actually, there is a difficulty with this particular point, because when writing this I have to consider whether I understand the word "meaning" in the same way as you, the reader. If I try to clarify the word, I have to use other words. However, the problem will still exist, because the new words might also be understood differently by myself and the reader.

The basic words in this part of the book are *idea, description, explanation, meaning, and understanding*. Let us look at my understandings of these words.

I see an idea as a glimpse of something; a description, an explanation, a meaning, or something else. A description can be understood as a firmer "picture." It can also be regarded as a moving picture in that it contains all the qualities that correspond to the senses of seeing, hearing, smelling, tasting, and touching, and to sensations "inside" the body.

Explanation is regarded as how the "picture" can be understood. *Meaning* consists of descriptions and explanations, but is also something more, in the sense that the descriptions and explanations mean something to people. This meaning becomes the basis for how a person relates to the given content in the dialogue, in that it describes and explains some kind of action. The word understanding is very similar to that of meaning. In this text, definition is regarded as description plus explanation. Meaning is thus more than definition—it is the definition plus the personal component of the definer.

I have found it useful to use this approach, with the above question areas, in my supervision groups. It helps when talking about the choices that are available and agreeing on the relationships and contexts with group members in supervision sessions.

For example, if one member of the supervision group interviews the therapist who wants to present the case for the other members to later reflect on, instead of encouraging the therapist to present his or her own views (which might lead to the team accepting her/his definition of the problem or his/her construction of "reality"), the interviewer starts by asking questions such as:

"Which concerns led you to discuss this case?"

"Which dilemmas do you face in your work with this family, couple, or person?"

"What understanding or explanations do you have about these dilemmas?"

The two centres in the green ellipse are set by the interviewer and the therapist, and their mutual dialogue is then created within the green elliptical line on the map. Other team members remain silent, listening, in the white hermeneutic area, perhaps noting their own thoughts and being aware of their own inner emerging images during the dialogue. They inhabit the position of keeping the observer's inner focus on the concerns that led the therapist to the actual presentation. The interviewer continues with additional dialogical questions while the others listen and generate their own ideas and questions, which are then reflected back to the therapist and interviewer. The therapist is given an opportunity to comment on any of the ideas that s/he finds interesting. Sometimes the two-person dialogue continues, and sometimes there is a reflective discussion among the group members. The supervisor's responsibility is to ensure that the focus is either maintained or changed to a more open reflection on the different meta-levels of professional inner and outer relationships and to note the different reflections of the team members.

When using this model, the therapist being interviewed often reports the positive feeling of not being bombarded by questions from colleagues who are eager to participate and help. The relational questioning by one person has more continuity, and the therapist feels less pulled in different directions. The nonjudgmental and tentative reflections also allow awkward issues to be broached, such as whether there is any connection between the case and the therapist's own life, or whether there are other potential isomorphs. The therapist being interviewed feels less defensive, because s/he does not have to respond directly to any of the reflecting team's comments, but is free to respond to whatever s/he wants.

CASE EXAMPLE

During supervision work with a team of family therapists, two colleagues (a male and a female) asked the group for ideas about how they could best proceed in their work with a couple. Peter had originally seen the couple together, but after three sessions the wife, who was recovering from her second cancer operation, decided not to continue with couple therapy for the time being. Instead, she asked to see a female therapist for individual sessions, citing a need to work on her own issues. Peter agreed to refer the wife to a female colleague,

Elisabeth, who had extensive experience with cancer patients. The husband wanted to continue seeing Peter individually until the couple therapy resumed. Due to the husband's anxious and intrusive style, the two therapists agreed that it was important to have clear boundaries for the individual therapies.

The husband at first encouraged the wife's separate therapy. However, as she became increasingly desperate about the marriage, he began to tell Peter that his wife was "lying" to Elisabeth and began anxiously pushing Peter to tell Elisabeth his side of the story so that she had the "full picture." He also began complaining to Peter that his wife was doing certain things because "Elisabeth told her to do it," which made Peter feel protective of Elisabeth and her reputation as a therapist. Under these conflicting pressures, Peter tried to talk to Elisabeth about how the therapy with the wife was progressing and asked whether she thought couple therapy should be resumed. Elisabeth, who had just learned that the wife had been sexually abused as a child, felt even more strongly that the wife's boundaries should be respected, and experienced Peter's questions as a violation of the boundaries around her therapy with this client. She believed that, given the wife's lifelong experience of being violated, the wife should be the one to decide when to resume couple therapy. She felt strongly that it would be a therapeutic mistake to push the wife into couple therapy and told Peter this. She also wondered whether, in a covert way, Peter was questioning her competence as a therapist.

Elisabeth turned to another team member, a woman, for several informal consultations about the case. Peter also talked to this woman in an attempt to clarify his concerns and perhaps gain her support for renewing couple therapy. The female colleague viewed what was happening between the two therapists as isomorphic to the couple's "dance," pointed this out to Peter, and wondered why he was pushing so hard for couple therapy when, ordinarily, he would view this as a choice for the couple to make jointly. She also wondered if he would deal with the husband's anxiety differently if the wife was seeing a therapist from a different agency. Although Peter acknowledged that he wouldn't, he was frustrated about the two women colleagues' ideas because he felt that the husband had no "voice" or way of influencing his wife.

A crisis developed when the wife began to have suicidal thoughts. Both therapists became very anxious and asked to present the case at the team's supervision group. As the supervising consultant, I suggested using content in the blue frame, which we then agreed on. The result was that I first formed an elliptical dialogue with the female colleague who had been consulting Elisabeth and Peter, and then formed an elliptical dialogue with Elisabeth and Peter individually. The other team members observed the various dialogues by reflecting on and listening to them. The idea was that this whole energized elliptical dialogic area, including the blue frame, the ego-self positions within the green elliptical line, and the inhabited white space, would form a mercurial field that could generate new possible perspectives.

I began by asking the consulting colleague about her role and her inner thoughts and images, using questions like: "How did you become involved in this case? How would you describe the dilemma from Peter's and Elisabeth's perspectives? Is it similar or different? How do you see the connection between Elisabeth and the wife? How do you see the bond between Peter and the husband? Are there similar issues between Elisabeth and Peter? How would you explain Peter's frustration? Does the fact that Peter feels that he has not been "heard" by the two female team members indicate underlying gender issues in the team?"

Other questions focused on whether the wife's suicidal tendency made the therapists anxious and whether any other systems were involved. After this first elliptical dialogue, Peter and Elisabeth were able to enter the elliptical dialogue in turn and add their own narratives, using the ideas and comments that had arisen in the dialogues with me.

A considerable amount of information, feelings, and emerging experiences was generated in the different elliptical dialogues with each of the people involved and in the meta-level of the larger dialogical context within the containing blue frame. Interesting factors in the dialogues were that both the wife and the female therapist had had cancer, the husband and the male therapist had similar ways of dealing with anxiety, the relationship between Peter and Elisabeth was hierarchical when the female therapist was an intern three years previously, but had changed as the therapist gained confidence in her own skills and ideas. The relationship between the husband and wife, which became stronger during the latter's recovery from the first cancer operation, had originally been hierarchical in the sense that the wife was totally dependent on her husband for nurture and support. However, the wife's need for the husband to be a caretaker had lessened as she became more successful in her professional work. The threat of suicide created additional issues: one of Elisabeth's former clients had recently committed suicide, and Peter was concerned that the husband, who was already angry at Elisabeth, would sue if the wife took such action.

After the three elliptical dialogues, the other members of the team reflected and amplified on all the multiple levels and views that had emerged, while their three colleagues listened. In this context, the other team members moved with me along the green elliptical line, which meant that this area consisted of myself plus four team members. In this process, my task was to collect and clarify each team member's reflections and write a few significant words on the whiteboard, while the three therapists (the consultant therapist, Elisabeth and Peter) listened, taking the observant reflecting position in the whole elliptical dialogic system. In their reflections, the team members were able to highlight both the similarities and differences between the couples, which, in turn, helped the therapists to make clearer distinctions between themselves and the couple. Elisabeth, who up to this point had been powerfully caught up in the similarities, described listening to this part of the reflecting dialogue as especially helpful. She suddenly became clearer about all the ways in which she and Peter were not like the couple under therapy. For Peter, who felt that he had made a "mistake" by becoming drawn into siding with the husband's views, listened objectively to the team members' reflections, which made him feel less defensive. He felt that his position had been "heard" and understood and was struck by several of the reflections from the team members that his "intrusiveness" stemmed from his protective concern for Elisabeth. In the reflecting dialogue with the team members, they also raised some interesting questions about all the various relationships, for example, about whether the disagreements about the case reflected underlying gender issues. This also led to a unique joint reflection among all the members of the team on how they expressed anger and frustration with each other and how they reacted to feedback.

With this case example of how the model of the elliptical dialogue can be used in supervision together with the opening explorative fields or areas of questions, the idea is to demonstrate that the model of the elliptical dialogue can be used in different settings and is portable. It can be useful for creating a space and slowing things down so that the psyche can work more freely and respond to the hints, sparks, and tentative reflections that emerge. In other words, it allows inner changes, bodily sensations, and images to come to the fore and be made clearer. It also allows the self area and the archetypal images to rise in every participant, regardless of where in the elliptical dialogue they are. The structure of the elliptical dialogue can serve as a containing hermeneutical vessel for the strong tensions that arise between opposites and let them emerge, grow, and develop in a synthesising way in each participant in the elliptical dialogue.

PART I
THE ELLIPTICAL DIALOGUE

3. The elliptical dialogue and its limitations

Bateson (1979/2002, 1987/2005) and Jung (1961/1989, 2009) have drawn our attention to the fact that we see a phenomenon as different from its background. This comes close to what Wittgenstein (1961/2005) points to in his famous sentence as "*the limits of my language means the limits of my world.*" The map and territory of the elliptical dialogue and the model's reciprocity between theory and practice are important aspects. In order for it to be successful, it needs to be used in the appropriate way and in the appropriate conditions.

For Bateson, Jung, and Wittgenstein, limitation as restriction was also essential and was connected with the need to make distinctions, create differences, and outline context. Relating to the concept of Creatura and Pleroma, in Jung's *Septem Sermones ad Mortuos* (Jung 1961/2009) he insists on the contrast between Pleroma and Creatura (1916/1961/1989) or Creation (2009). On the one hand, Pleroma is both nothingness and fullness, which implies that thinking and being both cease because the eternal and endless have no qualities. This domain is governed by forces and impacts; a kind of cosmological undifferentiated soup where everything is mixed up in nothingness and fullness. It is fruitless to think of the Pleroma because this would mean self-dissolution (Jung 2009 p 347.) Creation, on the other hand, is the domain governed by distinctions and differences. These two concepts are fundamental for Bateson, Jung and Wittgenstein, especially when the latter creates his concept of the limits of language and that the world shows itself in the limits of language (Wittgenstein 1961/2005 p. 101 – 103 §5.6 – 5.641). For Bateson, the two sets of concepts match in the sense that there can only be maps in Creatura/Creation. His conclusion is that what gets from territory to map is *news of difference*. This news of difference was for him a synonym for information. He also could link this train of thought to what had been described in cybernetics as linked processes of feedback, reciprocity and resilience. In his thinking, mental processes could be defined as systemic. This has implications for how language is used and how sensitive we are to bodily sensations when using the structure of the elliptical dialogue.

For Jung it is essential to move toward differentiation, with the opposites ever present in our psyche as inner and outer realities. He likened it to using our two hands and two legs to move and walk rhythmically with our bodies. If we did not, he was convinced that:

> "We fall into the Pleroma itself and cease to be created beings. We lapse into dissolution in nothingness. This is the death of the creature. Therefore we die to the same extent that we do not differentiate. Hence the creature's essence strives toward differentiation and struggles against primeval, perilous sameness. This is called the *principium individuationis*. This principle is the essence of the creature. From this you can see why non-differentiation and non-distinction pose a great danger to the creature" (Jung 2009 p. 347).

Individuation is essential in analytical psychology and is one of its cornerstones. In clinical reality it is also essential. When I was an analysand, I remember telling my analyst about a dream in which I was in danger of following a capsized ship, with my mother on board, down into the depths of the sea. When I described the dream, my analyst's reflection was: "Well, now you know the void is there, and you know the existence of your abysmal, you feel it, and you can see it. But that does not mean you are going to go down with it. It is there in you, like in all of us." This rather robust reflection enabled me see it as a healthy distinction and allowed me to become conscious of my own void and to make it clear and differentiate between what my position and what the dream wanted me to see. In this way, I was able to hold the Pleroma and Creatura within my ego-self axis both together and apart in a balanced movement. Now, when taking a clinical view of the dream, I think of different kinds of regressive work and the importance of the analyst's position when following or not following the analysand down into the darker areas. It is a distinction between malign and benign regression, where the regressive work must all the time have the individuation process as the leading star. Jung himself was never afraid of going down into his deep unconscious layers. In The Red Book, we can follow his journey into darkness and toward more conscious positions that enabled him to develop his psychoanalytical theory. What is important in his texts and the highly colored images is that he was always in contact with his I. He never became a total part of or swallowed up in all the archetypal images and living creatures he met. Individuation and the I are about differentiation: The dialogue among the I, the ego, and the deep layers of the self, as it presents itself in archetypal dreams, images, and fantasies is not about dwelling and making a living there. That is why pleroma is linked to creatura and creation and why Jung also in his categories of instincts includes creativity and reflection as two of the five basic instincts (hunger, sexuality, activity, reflection, and creativity) of our psyche.

CHANGE AND EXCHANGE

Change can be both limitation and evolution. The first type of change relates to our actions (behaviour) when change is instructed from the outside. The other change comes from inside, where the actions, namely the sensing and intuition, feeling and thinking aspects, are widened. It comes when the ego-self axis is both vertical and horizontal in a transcendent movement from a deep connection with the unconscious layers to the conscious balanced layers; when the elliptical dialogue is both balanced and challenged in a way that is experienced as promoting growth.

The first kind of change is experienced as a threat to a person's integrity. In order to defend his or her integrity, the person shuts the imposing or instructing act out. In this process of closing off, the person limits the repertoire of being and the flow between the unconscious and consciousness. This limitation may satisfy the instructor if the limitation stops the behavior the instructor has defined as unwanted. Here it is important to note that these instructions easily contribute to limiting action and thereby the corresponding aspects of intuition, sensing, feeling and thinking. Such restraints, which are more or less predictable, correspond to the idea that a person can be steered by another. Instructions like this lead to intimidation, which is very different from intimacy. They also lead to the psyche understanding that psychic energy has not stopped but is supressed at another level but is nevertheless always present. These changes can be experienced as momentary relief. However, energy often pops up again from the unconscious and demands to be worked through. Sometimes these intimidations are surprising and sometimes very obvious. This is usually when the elliptical dialogue breaks down. When these ruptures occur, the most important thing to do is to be brave enough to look at what happened in the breakdown, enter into it, explore what happened there, see whether a reciprocal dialogue is possible, and work through the breakdown with the aid of mutual feedback. This process can increase our awareness of the limits of the unique dialogue we are participating in. The multiple layers in these kinds of ruptures are examined in the clinical part II of this book.

The second kind of change occurs when two or more people can exchange ideas and respect each other's point of view. Under such circumstances, new ideas can emerge. Such change evolves and cannot be predicted. Change like this has its own route and time. It is transformation. Thus, change can either limit or expand the ability to describe or explain being in the world and the different relationships encountered.

An example may clarify this. When we hold a little baby in our arms, we are sometimes blessed with the child's laughter. Its whole body laughs, as does our own. The laughing movement is top to toe. Even the baby's toes and fingers laugh. Then the child grows and starts to walk. The upright position perhaps limits the feet and toes taking part in the laughing movement. As the child grows, he or she may be taught that certain ways of laughing are more appropriate than others. In adolescence, he or she might learn that there are things you simply do not laugh at and that even smiling is to be controlled.

The point here is that we all have the potential to let the laughing movement reach and move the body's extremities, like the fingertips and toes. The possibilities only tend to be limited over time, as habits, customs, and so on are introduced. We also have the potential to shut down the laughing movement. If an unpleasant person is close, our smile, which has previously included our eyes, may stop at the lips. The unused smiles and laughs lie there, sleeping, waiting.

How can we create a togetherness that turns smiles and laughter into possibilities for freedom? Words and questions are often used to facilitate this. Exchanges of ideas with others can create new forms of laughter, such as through writing, painting, dancing, or singing.

THE FUNDAMENTAL RIGHT TO SAY 'NO'

But saying "no" is fundamental. Since the too unusual might threaten a person's integrity, it is imperative to organize the work in such a way that those who come for analysis, psychotherapy, and supervision have an ongoing opportunity to say no to an ongoing dialogue and its content and context. In this sense, saying "no" to the elliptical dialogue can mean that the dialogue in itself is not an option for the participating members. The best way of avoiding any unspoken "no" is to allow a dialogue about the ongoing dialogue to become part of the dialogue. Including words such as "like" and "comfortable" in the questions could be helpful in this respect: "How would you like to use the session?" "What would you feel most comfortable with?"

Every dialogue challenges our sensitivity to pick up on all the small bodily utterings that indicate discomfort or dislike. One of the everyday questions that might be posed at the end of a dialogue could be: "How do you feel about today's dialogue?" A question like this also addresses the caring and upholding of the unique relationship between sessions and points toward an image of the elliptical dialogue that we can all carry with us.

PART II
THE ELLIPTICAL DIALOGUE
AND TRANSFORMATION IN
JUNGIAN PSYCHOANALYSIS
– THE CLINICAL PART

4. The elliptical dialogue and individuation

Woman in Blue Reading a Letter 1663 – 1664.
Jan Vermeer (1632-1675.)
Copyright public domain Rijksmuseum Amsterdam

The blue frame in the map is here first seen as a container of some of the general perspectives from depth psychology and as individuation within life cycle transformations. I introduced Part I with illustrations by Vermeer picturing tools and instruments for navigation in the heavens and on Earth. There, the gaze of the astronomer and the geographer can be followed to other more unknown fields. In Part II, I turn to the clinical usefulness of the elliptical dialogue and illustrate this with another Vermeer painting, this time of a woman receiving external and internal messages. The blue frame in the elliptical dialogue will here be filled with some background perspectives from depths psychology and mainly from analytical psychology. These perspectives are meant to highlight some important conditions for growth and development for us as individual beings and for growth in close relationships. They form the background understanding for the clinical specific narrative to come.

Psychological theorists and pioneers like C. G. Jung also made maps of inner landscapes, the human psyche, and analytic relationships. We need maps and instruments for navigation and travel. They can be essential for survival in some circumstances. They are also necessary for staying on course. But an instrument or map is not a living thing in itself. They need a user and the user's skills and abilities to handle the instrument with care, judgment, and discrimination.

Jung's map of the human psyche is called analytical psychology. It is a fascinating map that not only consists of theoretical formulations, but also of encounters with children, dragons, monsters, unicorns, birds, heroes, magicians, demons, and the divine child, as Jung recounts in *The Red Book* (2009.) However, without the traveler, this map would be lifeless.

In my personal journey, Jung's map has helped me to set up my inner psychic landmarks. Through my own encounters with the unconscious and consciousness in my analytical journey, I have gained firsthand experience of my inner and outer spaces. This has helped me recognize my limits as well as my possibilities for growth and creativity. This firsthand knowledge has been made possible by journeying into the dark areas of the psyche. What we each find in the individuation journey will not be identical, exactly resemble the map, or respond in the same way to navigational instruments. The map is not the territory and never can be, even though it is tempting to rely on technology and tools for our desired goals and destinations in life. Our personal life is our own, and we embark on our individuation journeys from the very moment of birth, or even before…

Wer zeigt ein Kind, so wie es steht? Wer stellt
es ins Gestirn und giebt das Maß des Abstands
Ihm die Hand?

Who shows a child, just as they are? Who sets it
in its constellation, and gives the measure
of distance into its hand?

Vem ger oss barnet som det är? Vem ställer
det i dess stjärnbild, lägger avstånds mått
uti dess hand?

(Rainer Maria Rilke (1875 – 1926.)
www.poetryintranslation.com
The Duino Elegies, The Fourth Elegy.)

In this poem, Rilke gives the spiritual and existential dimension of the entrance of the child into the world. This entrance is not a matter of choice but of being. We cannot fully influence our lives or choose our parents and first environment. But we are equipped with psychic conditions allowing us to grow far beyond what we perhaps can imagine. This individuation journey can be seen as a movement and creation toward consciousness. In life, in relationships, and within ourselves, there is potential for forming an image of myself in dialogue with the world.

The individuation process lies at the centre of Jung's dynamic model of the psyche. It is to be understood as a never-ending movement between the world and the psyche, I and You, and the inner and outer reality. From the beginning of our individual lives to the final threshold, we are connected to and in relationship with the inner world of the unknown. Individuation is one of the basic cornerstones of analytical psychology. Many Jungian analysts have shared their own images of the individuation process and its place in analytical psychology. In this section, I rely on the work of Jungian analysts that I have found helpful. One of these analysts is Erich Neumann (1905-1960), who developed Jung's understanding and systematized his theory. Neumann's notion of the formation of the ego-self axis in the second half of life is critically important. Here he links the development of the ego-self to creativity (Neumann 1969/1990 *Depth Psychology and a New Ethic*, 1973/1990 *The Child Neumann* 1989 *The Place of Creation*). Another presenter of Jungian analytical psychology is Murray Stein, whose lectures and books give a full picture of how relevant, important, and fresh analytical psychology is for understanding ourselves as individuals and our connection to the world (Stein 1998/2006 *Jung's Map of the Soul*, 2014 *Minding the Self*, 2015 *Soul – Treatment and Recovery*).

But let us begin with Jung's own words: "Wholeness is a combination of I and You, and these show themselves to be parts of a transcendent unity whose nature can only be grasped symbolically…" (Jung CW 16 § 454). In a footnote, Jung explains further: "Hence wholeness is the product of an intrapsychic process which depends essentially on the relation of one individual to another. Relationship paves the way for individuation and makes it possible, but is itself no proof of wholeness" (Jung CW 16 § 454 footnote 16). This quotation is found in one of Jung's most important texts, *The Psychology of the Transference*, where we can read about his understanding of the relationship in the psychotherapeutic setting. The clinical perspective is based on archetypal images from the place in which Jung meets the ancient Gnostics and medieval alchemists. This makes the individuation journey relevant for human development as a whole and for our own analytical journeys. Based on my understanding of these texts, I will now link the elliptical dialogue to our individuation as human beings.

How did we become human in the first place? The question of human origins has never ceased to fascinate me. How did humans learn to live, work together, and love? In his book, *Dawn over the Kalahari: How Humans Became Humans* (2005/2011), Lasse Berg gives us a fascinating perspective of human development. He especially notes our curiosity and our ability as storytellers, relating to others the experiences of hunters and gatherers. Generosity and open-handedness are also important values for survival and cooperation. Worth noting is our invention of the bag as a form for containment, which includes everything from a plaited basket made from nature's resources to our modern-day bags. In the bag, we carry and collect. It is a container that can be opened and closed, used to transport things, and is mobile in that its contents can be shared with others in different places. All these functions also facilitate the development of structures and the formation of relationships.

The archetypal unit for survival is the mother-child and male-female-child triangle. While this unit can have different constellations and developmental stages, it is our experience of relationships in the family setting that we form profound images and acquire symbols for our life narratives. Families often share the task of protecting and fostering the children, but it is within these family relationships that emotional bonds are created that will prepare children for life outside the family unit and also prepare parents for life when the children have left the nest and the transition back to being a couple. How will they rub shoulders again when they no longer have responsibility for their offspring? This transition may also involve their children continuing to fly in and out of the nest before finally settling in their own lives. This constitutes an important individuation development for all members of the family. How this can be made constructive will depend on the relational bonds and dialogues that have been set up and carried out within the family unit.

Sigmund Freud (1856-1939) and Carl Gustav Jung (1875-1961) are the two pioneers of psychoanalysis. Their clinical experience developed by listening to and analyzing their patients' narratives, which enabled them to refine their theories of psychic development. They were both deeply interested in the libido energy of the individual. Freud regarded libido as a psychosexual development and aggression as self- and power-assertion. He called the two basic principles Eros and Thanatos in his theory of personality formation. Jung regarded the concept of libido as psychic energy and a fundamental life force. For him, symbols, created in the unconscious and expressed in dreams, enabled the individual psyche to develop and become whole. This energy for wholeness is the individuation principle in analytical psychology.

Pioneer work on personality development was conducted by Erich Neumann. He had been trained in philosophy and medicine and, as a psychoanalyst, studied with C. G. Jung in Zürich and had his practice in Tel Aviv. His book *The Child* examines the structure and relational dynamics of the ego and its individuality.

Murray Stein is a contemporary psychoanalyst who works and writes in the tradition of analytical psychology. His writings (1998/2006, 2010, 2014, 2015) constitute a deep and comprehensive presentation of modern analytical psychology.

Object relations theory, with its representatives Melanie Klein (1882-1960), Ronald D. Fairbairn (1889-1964) and Donald W. Winnicott (1896-1971), focuses on the relationship between the individual and significant important others. How these relationships develop can be important for the individual's sense of self and attitude to the surrounding world.

In contemporary infant research, Daniel N. Stern (1934-2012) is important for his studies in the mother-infant relationship. Building on Kohut (1971) and his self psychology, Stern's contributions are important for the preverbal experience of self. He emphasizes the nonverbal interplay—the dialogue—between parent and child, and that this is the child's actual mother tongue.

Edward Tronick (2007) is an American developmental psychologist who studies infants and their caregivers in interaction. He is best-known for his Still Face Paradigm. (https://www.youtube.com/watch?v=bG89Qxw30BM)

The study involves children of different ages and looks at how the still face affects them emotionally. When the connection between an infant and caregiver is broken, the infant tries to engage the caregiver, and if there is no response, pulls back—first physically and then emotionally. Another response is to try to engage the caregiver by repeatedly asking, calling, shouting, and finally being physical in a desperate attempt to re-engage the caregiver. Tronick underlines the significance of the resilience, i.e., that when the connection is regained and interaction can continue. He also says that human beings go in and out of sync with each other, which is the normal interactive pattern. However, when young children are repeatedly exposed to the still face without sufficient reconnection for safety and security, they risk remaining in an insecure liminal space and becoming anxious. This is common in our consulting rooms too. Therefore, as a psychotherapist, consciously attending to facial movements, gazes and the physical space of the room is important.

This became very clear in my work with Björn and at the theoretical level connects to affect theory and the analytical psychology that arises from Jung's formulation of the five instincts in his 1936 Harvard Lecture, *Psychological Factors Determining Human Behaviour* (CW 8, § 232 – 262).

In analytical psychology, the self also has its grounds in the individual relationship, in the combination of I and You. But the Jungian self concept also points to a wider meaning that goes beneath and beyond our personal life situation. It wants to illuminate the relationship of the ego to the collective unconscious as it is rooted in myths and symbols, but also to the ego connection of the spiritual aspect of our lives. The consciousness of this self archetype is central in Jungian psychoanalytical work, and we can follow its development in Björn's images and words. But first let us look at the origins of analytical psychology and follow the development of contemporary formulations and an understanding of the self.

CREATING SPACE FOR THE SELF

It is interesting to note that at the same time as Jung was working on *The Red Book*, he also was working on Psychological Types. These two texts can be seen as both an expression of his own experience of the self and his formulation of the theoretical perspective of the self. Jung intensely experienced the self, the ego, the different archetypes, the symbols, and his individuation journey when painting and when writing *The Red Book*. In *Psychological Types*, he developed the first comprehensive formulations of analytical psychology by defining the self:

"46. SELF. As an empirical concept, the self incorporates the entire range of psychic phenomena. It expresses the unity of the personality as a whole. But in terms of the total personality, due to its unconscious component, it can only be partly conscious. The concept of the self is thus only potentially empirical and to that extent a postulate. In other words, it encompasses both the experienceable and the inexperienceable (or the not yet experienced). It shares these qualities with scientific concepts that are more names than ideas. In so far as psychic totality, consisting of both conscious and unconscious contents, is a *postulate*, it is a transcendental concept, because it presupposes the existence of unconscious factors on empirical grounds and thus characterizes an entity that can be described in part but to all intents and purposes is unknowable and unlimitable.

Just as conscious and unconscious phenomena are encountered in practice, the self as a psychic totality has both a conscious and an unconscious aspect. Empirically, the self appears in dreams, myths, and fairy tales in the shape of a "supraordinate personality" (V. EGO), such as a king, hero, prophet, saviour and so on or in form of a totality symbol, such as a circle, square, *quadratura circuli*, cross etc. When it represents a *complexio oppositorium*, or union of opposites, it can also appear as a united duality, for instance in the form of tao as the interplay of *yang* and *yin*, the hostile brother, the hero and his adversary (arch-enemy, dragon), Faust, Mephistopheles etc. Thus, empirically, the self appears as a play of light and shadow, albeit conceived as a totality and unity in which the opposites are united. As such a concept is irrepresentable—*tertium non datur*—it is transcendental in this respect too. Logically, it would be a vain speculation if it did not designate empirically occurring symbols of unity.

The self is not a philosophical idea because it does not predicate its own existence, i.e. does not hypostatize itself. From an intellectual point of view it is just a working hypothesis. Its empirical symbols, on the other hand, often possess a distinct *numinosity*, i.e. an a priori emotional value, as in the case of the mandala "Deus est circulus…, the Pythagorean tetractys, the quarternity etc. It thus proves to be an *archetypal idea (v. Idea; Image)*, which differs from the idea of the kind in that it occupies a central position that befits its content and its numinosity." (CW 6 §§ 789-791).

When Jung defines the self, he makes it clear that it is a transcendental concept that cannot be fully grasped by the ego and the intellect, but yet constitutes the archetypal basis for the psyche to express itself and create concepts. He focuses on the wholeness of the conscious and unconscious components of our personality. Therefore, the images produced by the psyche tend to point to this totality from the perspective of the union of opposites. There is also a strong affect in these images, as in Björn's Rottweiler dream. These images are felt within the body and remain there for a long time, perhaps even a lifetime. In this sense, they bring order or ordering in situations where the psyche is threatened by chaos and instability. The Red Book stems from Jung's own struggle with inner forces that challenged his mental health. It is well-known that he practiced yoga meditations, with breathing, painting, active imagination, creative writing, and playing with stones as channels for holding and containing his psychic energy and avoiding the risk of overflow. The practical exercises he did served to create a relationship and dialogue among the ego, the I and the self. This enabled the transcendental power of self energies and images to emerge and reach a higher degree of consciousness. These models were later used with patients, for example, with a Scandinavian woman (Jung CW 9i), in a study of the process of individuation. We can also easily relate to them as expressive art therapy, which were developed further by others.

As indicated earlier, Jung's ideas and psychology were later developed by Erich Neumann. Jung was asked to write the foreword for Neumann's The Origins and the History of Consciousness (Neumann 1954). Here Jung makes it clear that "the most valuable aspect of the work is the fundamental contribution it makes to a psychology of the unconscious. The author has placed the concepts of analytical psychology—which for many people are so bewildering—on a firm evolutionary basis and erected upon this a comprehensive structure in which the empirical forms of thought find their rightful place." Erich Neumann builds on the fundamental concepts of analytical psychology in many ways. Here we will especially consider the development of the ego-self axis, both from the first half of life and the second.

Neumann's contribution to developmental child psychology is based on his theoretical thinking and clinical experience from his practice in Tel Aviv, where he lived until his death in 1960. In Neumann's posthumously published The Child (Neumann 1973), this development is described as being from the intrauterine embryonic phase, where the embryo is integrated psychically and physically with the mother's body, to the post-uterine embryonic phase, in which the child enters into human society and the unique primal relationship with its parents. In this close relationship with the parent the ego-self axis slowly begins to form. However, the total personality and its directing centre, the self, exists before the ego takes shape and develops into a centre of consciousness. In this first phase of reality, the embryo and the mother are fused in one body.

Parents often have a fantasy in their inner world of giving the embryo an identity and can also listen to the fetal heartbeat when going to the prenatal clinic for checkups. The two hearts in one body signals the beginning of a relationship with the expected child. From the child's perspective, Neumann selects the term uroboric for this initial pre-ego state. By using the symbol of the uroboros, the circular snake touching its tail and "eating" it, he wants to elucidate the oppositionless unity of this psychic reality for the embryo—fetus—child. In this phase, it is the mother's body that is the world in which the child lives. The mother's body holds the regulation of the child's organism. The child's perceiving consciousness is not yet ego-centered, and Neumann calls this phase the body-self. The self is here grounded in the biopsychic unity in the mother's body. Two hearts beat in one body.

With birth, the child's bond with the mother is partly preserved, although now the other parent is also an individual who has to be allowed let into the primal relationship. In terms of the elliptical dialogue, the mother's ego-self axis is challenged to become transcendent and exercise flexibility. The birthing mother is challenged to open up her body to physical pain in order to give birth to the child. In the mother's psychic reality, she is in many ways regressed. It is well-known that pregnant mothers-to-be come close to their relationship with their own mothers and that at the end of pregnancy it is important to build the nest. The mother's ego-self axis is highly active, both concerning the personal conscious and unconscious reality but also in the collective conscious and unconscious reality. Neumann would here apply his second half model of ego self-development (Neumann 1989) as outlined in *The Psyche and the Transformation of the Reality Planes: A Metapsychological Essay*.

In the elliptical dialogue model, the mother and the newborn child have totally different positions, while the mother and the other parent have a one-sided responsibility for the relationship and bond with the newborn child. The other parent's ego-self axis is also challenged, perhaps to become a more stable holding person for the mother-child unity, but also to be able to step into this unity and participate in it. The other parent has to hold both the outer and inner reality planes and the osmotic transparence between the reality planes. In Neumann's model for the development of the ego-self axis, in the second half of life, he suggests that the self field is superior, but he places it as a ground below the archetypal field in the model. The self field moves with growing constellation of consciousness toward the archetypal field, and simultaneously the ego moves toward a more solid ego-self constellation. Fully developed, this leads toward a centering of the personality and an ability for the ego-self axis to hold a unity between psyche and world into one experience of a reality plane as one but not fused. (Neumann 1989 p. 19.)

When this model is transformed to the newborn family triad, one can say that all three participants—the child, the mother and the other parent—are thus in totally different ego-self positions and stages of development. For the mother parent and the father parent, the challenge of holding and containing the relationship between each other and the newborn child is filled with wonder. The experience and image of the vulnerable yet energetic child go right to our hearts, touch us deeply and stir up our innermost instincts. The term used in analytical psychology for this energetic field is participation mystique. Jung borrowed this term from the French anthropologist Levy-Bruhl, and Neumann makes it relevant when describing how in the deeper layers of the personality polarization becomes invalid. In certain states of development and deep relationship, outer reality is experienced as inner reality, and inner reality is experienced as outer reality. It is an identification between an individual's consciousness and the surrounding world, but without any awareness of being in this state. It is pure natural being. Consciousness and the other is identified as mysteriously whole. This forms the basis for the child's experience of being and becoming in the world and for the parents' ability to meet the child's fundamental needs for safety and security. There is also an underlying power at work in analytical experience and perhaps more so in those moments of encounter that are so numinous (from lat. *numen* "divine will") with a strong spiritual quality but yet difficult to put into words. This is constituted from the language of being and instincts. Neumann described the energies at work in this development of individuation as *centroversion* and *automorphism*. Both energies are at work throughout the life cycle and postulate individuation and oscillate between extraversion and introversion. Neumann writes:

"Whereas the concept of centroversion applies to the interrelation of the personality centres, the concept of automorphism embraces the development not so much of the psychic centres as of the psychic systems: consciousness and the unconscious. It concerns their relation to one another; for example, the compensatory relation of the unconscious to consciousness, and also the process that takes place only in the unconscious or only in consciousness but serve the development of the personality as a whole" (Neumann The Child p. 9-10).

In the first half of life, the centroversion as energy and movement helps to form the centre of consciousness and build the ego-complex. This can be seen as a synthesising movement as a result of both extraversion and introversion in relationship to oneself and to the other, for example the parents, other children, and people with whom the growing individual forms relationships. Automorphism points to the specific and unique tendency to fulfill the individual's potential. In this sense, we can say that we are structurally determined to develop within our community but, if necessary, in opposition to our context. It points toward the uniqueness of each individual and to the various expressions of this uniqueness. This can sometimes become a source of conflict in a family system if a child does not meet accepted norms or is regarded as conforming to the system. For example, in Björn's family, he was expected to almost behave like a self-supporting little soldier. This proved impossible for him with his strong creative energy and talent for writing and drawing, and his sensitive needs for close relationships. He was structurally determined to express his unique individuality, although in another family system, he may have been encouraged to express his creative skills. This energy could not be totally supressed within him or within the family. It is an example of the automorphism and unique tendency to come into being and active doing. It is impossible to stop. Libido as a life force continues, even in times of suffering, loss, and abandonment. Just as the day breaks through and the blue hour appears each morning, the self field is at work within and in our relationships.

As our ego-self axis begins to grow and become profiled, we are more able to cope with different transitions of life and our various relationships. This also forms the basis for decisions and the ability to make choices. Of course, this differs depending on where we are in our individuation process and on genetic, physical, and psychological prerequisites.

The dramatic event when Odysseus returns to Ithaka is an example of this. I read and perceive Homer's *Odyssey* as a mythological narrative of relational individuation from the masculine, the feminine, and the child's perspectives. It is rich and adventurous, it twists and turns for all participants, its energy is constructive and destructive, and the ego complexes are challenged for the wife and mother, Penelope, for the husband and father, Odysseus, and the son, Telemachos. Questions abound. Who is the enemy, whom can I rely on, what is necessary to offer, what do I have to let go of, and what do I have to achieve? What are the losses, pain, and sorrows? When is the time for conflict, struggle, endurance, and waiting? When do love and relationship develop, and what are the limits of the coniunctio movement and the separatio movement according to the elliptical dialogue? This episode explores the limits of the possibilities of dialogue.

Homer's *Odyssey* can be read as an archetypal individuation journey of family life and relationship. It contains narratives about the masculine hero energy of Odysseus developing as a father and an integrated man in contact with his anima, his contrasexual complex. It also contains narratives about the feminine-containing eros energy of Penelope and motherhood, and an integrated woman in contact with her animus, her contrasexual complex. From the growing child's perspective, Telemachos' task was to develop the ego-self axis by leaving home when his mother struggled with suitors and domesticity and, in that way, escaping threatened chaos and disintegration. It was not an easy and secure family life, but very recognizable in our contemporary world.

Only Odysseus himself could fire the arrow from his own bow and become the father and husband constellation in his family. The bow had been given to him by his friend Iphitus when they were boys. He only kept it at Ithaka, and it marks the moment when he is present as the father, husband, and master in his own house. The reunion comes alive for him, his child and his wife—his family—the archetypal family pattern of man, woman, and child. All Penelope's suitors had tried to fire the arrow through the handle-rings of the axes but had failed. Odysseus succeeded by combining himself, the bow, the fired arrow, and the given target of a new synthesised coniunctio relationship in his own house. A new balance was created at the cost of a battle with the predatory suitors. They had to be slaughtered, because in The Odyssey the suitors had taken over Odysseus' household in a perversion of the convention of xenia (the obligation to entertain and take care of outsiders). The suitors had no respect for this obligatory bond of solidarity between insiders and outsiders, the xenia, (Greek *xenos* "strange"). Their aim was to get their hands on its wealth and power and on Penelope as a projected unintegrated anima. This justified their deaths (Homer c 750-700BC/1991). Certain emotional behaviour is inconsistent with the creation of life and relationship in this context. After the massacre, Odysseus' home was cleaned with sulphur and fire. If we read Homer's *The Odyssey* as a symbolic and archetypal narrative of a relational life cycle perspective, we can create certain transitional points in the life cycle. It is also possible to create certain conditions for an elliptical dialogue in our consulting room and for an elliptical dialogue in the life cycle transition of man, woman, and child as archetypal symbols.

BEING ONESELF AND RELATING TO OTHER(S)— LIFE CYCLE TRANSFORMATIONS

In the following description of life cycle transitions, I underline the psychoanalytical pioneers and archetypal narratives and their relevance for the significant dialogues in the life cycle transformation.

In my mind, I sometimes imagine the energy of the individuation process as a vector, which in mathematics is often illustrated by an arrow, with its own energy and deep layers of the inner archetypal self field. If this energy is not related to in a way that is relevant in a person's present situation, the arrow does not point to the target necessary for transformation. The elliptical dialogue, with its words and sublingual processes, will thus be in a destructive and painful rupture, and the individuation process frozen and inhibited. We will close up in order to preserve our integrity. But even when circumstances are difficult or even dangerous, our instincts focus on survival and the preservation of life.

The illustration of the life cycle on page 99 is highly generalized and highlights crucial points where archetypal relational transformations come into focus from an existential perspective. Standing alone and being alone is a human existential condition. In the life cycle circle, it is possible to be in different places at the same time. For example, if you form a new family, you can at the same time have small children to look after, a passionate relationship to maintain, or teenage children to relate to from a former relationship and their struggles for individuality. Alternatively, after a separation that has been decided on and lived through either by agreement or after great conflict or the loss of a partner, you might find yourself being a single parent with children of different ages.

If we choose to enter the circle from the child's observing perspective, we might be born into a family with elder teenage siblings or a one-parent family and other significant adults in the periphery with a parental role. It is also important to see the feminine and masculine in every human being. In analytical psychology, these aspects are known as the animus and the anima: animus as the psychological contrasexual masculine ability in a woman and anima as the psychological contrasexual feminine ability in a man. We enter the world as individuals and exit it in the same way. However, relationships are important for survival and necessary for individuation. At every point of our life transformations, the elliptical dialogue is charged with energy to promote development; not only in our outer circumstances but also in our inner, dynamic relationships. During an analytical session with Björn, one of these life transformations came to the fore again as we worked with inner complexes that held us in their grip. Our psyche and minds have the amazing ability to relate and talk to our deceased loved ones at the same time as we experience their absence in our bones. This does not mean that we can cope with everything. Sometimes, life is too hard for that and from the outside can take the form of surrender or giving up. But that position might be the only one available to us at that particular time. We cannot control or choose actions or attitudes unless we can hold the ego-self axis fairly in balance. We are influenced by the ego-self axis in ways that we cannot imagine. Often, the unconscious is accompanied by a consciousness that is not yet clear to our ego consciousness. This can take the form of surprising actions, dreams, or fantasies that are connected to our life situations, even though this may not be apparent at first. But it is as though the unconscious gives us a sign that enables us to work out the meaning of these events — just as in my initial dream of the wolverine when I entered my own analysis (see Preface p. 7.) This energetic force coming from my self field was able to shoot the vector and arrow to make way for consciousness in my analytical work.

This, I would also say, is relevant for supervision based on analytical psychology. These moments and life transformations can be re-created by the mutual energetic self field in the elliptical dialogue and worked through in the analytical and supervisory relationship.

During supervisory work with a female psychotherapist working within a psychiatric clinic, this energetic arrow fired from self and archetypal field made itself visible during several sessions; the supervisee had an ongoing psychotherapeutic work with a female patient. The theme circulated around experienced anxiety in different forms, from turning dizzy when walking to inability to walk up and down stairs for fear of falling down. My supervisee herself then remembered her traumatic childhood experience when sleepwalking and falling out of the window from her room. She was in hospital for several weeks, and to everyone's great wonder and joy, she began to feel her sensory nerves and regained her ability to walk. She never fully understood what happened that night. She just woke up in the hospital bed paralyzed in her legs. During our supervision sessions, she had a dream about her fall. She saw herself climbing out of bed and experienced the fall from the window and felt herself lying in grass below. Simultaneously her patient began to walk on stairs and became able to go by bus and other public transportation. The patient's anxiety and dizziness was also connected to a childhood experience of being pushed into a ditch and, in a deeper sense, of being neglected by her parents. Now the ability to perceive the sensitivity from unconscious layers that emerged in these images and in the psychotherapist's dream can be seen as an experience of how the self field made itself visible in different relational settings and thus was made conscious in psychotherapy as well as in supervision. The arrow energy became like a compass needle that points toward the direction for individuation and deep transformation. This is just one experience of how the development of human consciousness can find its way up from deep layers in different planes until becoming visible in the united reality planes shared by

Family with young children → Family with teenage children → The couple "empy nest" → Alone → The couple → Family with young children

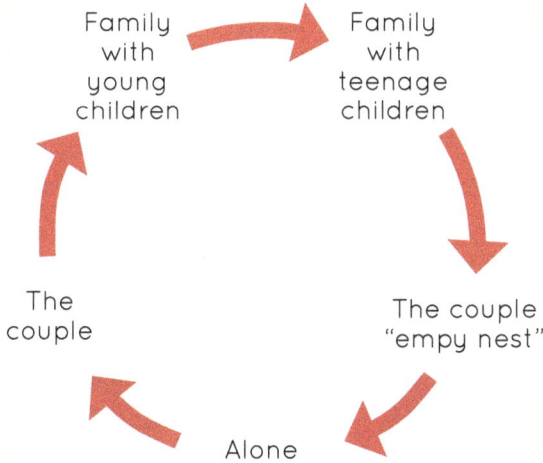

Life cycle transformation - Figure Created by Gunilla Midbøe

the patient—supervisee/psychotherapist and supervisor.

Using words and relational dynamics, we can tell our story, be listened to, and form a perhaps more coherent story in which emotions, affects, and pain can merge and be shared in the relationship with the other. This might not change what actually happens, but when seen in another light in an analytical relationship or supervision, it may be possible to continue one's life narrative but from another perspective. This participation and engagement does something profound with your inner and outer being. Neumann refers to this as extraneous knowledge (Neumann 1989 p. 6), i.e., a connecting field knowledge that emerges as part of a reality field. Knowledge itself is situated in this field and has its metaphysical unitary character. I suggest that these field knowledges are especially vibrant and dwell below the surface in the *abaissement du niveau mental*. Just as in the various life transformations, knowledge beneath the actual state of consciousness is available to the psyche.

When your own children are teenagers, it is likely that you will experience an inner contact with yourself as a teenager. An inner elliptical dialogue may emerge with your own parents, perhaps at the same time as you are struggling with your own teenager and reality of that situation. This can be both a resource and a pitfall. If you identify too much with your own teenager in the ego-self axis to the extent that you become fused and inflated by this energy, the elliptical dialogue with the teenager in the family can become too overidentified. The mature parent's task in this life transition is to keep his or her own memories and experiences of the teenage situation within bounds and at the same time maintain a strong ego position in the symbolic world with the teenager in the family. The extraneous field knowledge cooperates to push this knowledge to further consciousness and expand it.

On the previous page is a general illustration of the transitional points in a life cycle. In these suggested crucial transformations, the elliptical dialogue in the relational context can develop.

Relational words, acts and aims must all be possible in the elliptical dialogue. For the newborn child, this is a condition of life. When a baby is born, it comes without any conscious experience of structures and limits. The seeking that the baby expresses with its body is experienced by the mother when she puts her baby on her stomach. If the baby and mother are not too exhausted by the birth, the baby will start to crawl toward the breast, and the mother will reach out to hold him or her. If the other parent has been present at the birth, he/she may have been asked by the midwife to cut the baby's umbilical cord. This is common in our culture, but in some other cultures, the placenta is buried at the root of a special tree. This forms the beginning narrative of life told by ancestors, so that the grown-up individual will always know what the ground root for growth is. In a lecture (Henry Abramovitch Trieste, 3rd European Conference on Analytical Psychology, Thursday 27 August 2015) on working through culture, the question "Do you know where your placenta is?" was asked as an opener for connection and living in harmony with Earth and nature. This is also depicted in J. M. G. Le Clezio's novel *Désert* (1980).

Birth is a baby's first real struggle for survival and a total archetypal dependence that paves the way for the child's future ability to create close relationships. In order not to be abandoned, but be related to, the mother must be capable of creating the wholeness I and You. The bonds in the mother-infant dialogue are the gaze, the eye, and behaviour. This is a prelinguistic language that is generated by bodily reactions. The baby is held, cuddled, and in response, at least in the eyes of its parents, appears to be "really truly and objectively the most beautiful baby in the world!"

The focusing space between the mother's and the baby's eyes, including the feeding breast, creates an archetypal elliptical dialogue for further growth for mother, child, and other parent. This holding and space also exists, and is important, when for some reason breast-feeding is not possible. The other parent's position in the elliptical dialogue is that of confirming and holding the observer's participant position without being too jealous of the mother-and-baby dyad. This trialogue lays the foundation for the baby's feeling of safety and security. When Wittgenstein writes about language games, he says: "The origin and primitive form of the language game is a reaction; only from this can more complicated forms develop." (Wittgenstein 1980, p. 31) Wittgenstein explains that by primitive, he means that "this sort of behaviour is pre-linguistic: that a language game is based on it, that it is the prototype of a way of thinking and not the way of thought." In this respect, Wittgenstein's notion of intimate prelanguage action is similar to Bateson's and his idea of maintaining integrity and holding differences within the frame of a relationship.

A few weeks later in the mother-child-father development, the first smile and the peekaboo game contain the most basic language actions and words for the experience of differentiation and conjunction in the individuation process. This language game is played all over the world. At one level it can be experienced as a horrible game. The parent disappears from the child's sight. But then—"boo"—is suddenly present again. This can teach us something about the importance of holding polarities in a tension that does not break the elliptical dialogue. If the time between the "peek" and the "boo" is too long, the baby's face and yours will not be wreathed in smiles of recognition and reunion. If this is repeated too often, the child might feel abandoned and left out. Another variation of this face-to-face language is shown by Tronick in his still-face experiments. The mother in front of the baby is instructed to show a still face. After a while, the baby becomes worried, anxious, and actively tries to get the mother to react. When she does not, the baby gives up and seems depressed. When the mother again responds to the child, the interaction is retrieved, and the mother and child reunite in their common language. But if this is repeated too many times and with long intervals in between, the experience of separation is one of abandonment and being left out. This does not promote safe individuation language. Being able to give and let go at the right time is always a difficult balancing act. This is an archetypal situation of being in a close yet distant relationship but at the same time in a holding elliptical dialogue. When the "boo" comes and the inner sense of the other in the baby's ego-self axis is secured and unbroken, it determines how the analytical relationship can be created and how the participants can both hold and stand separation and reunion.

At every point of the life cycle transformation, there is a specific relational and dialogical challenge. This step is crucial if a couple are to transform from the passion of *falling* in love to meeting the challenge of becoming two separate individuals. The state of passion resembles the baby's first state, where the ego is embedded in the self but not yet differentiated. Here, I fall into the other's ego-self system and the other falls into mine. It is fusion and passion and a feeling of paradise. In Neumann's (1956) text about Amor and Psyche, Psyche is in this state in Eros' paradise and is instructed to not look at him whilst making love. This taboo has to be broken, and the seeing and awakening of consciousness is a necessary step for the couple to take, both in order to become individuated as a couple and to formulate their own needs. How much space and confirmation from the other is needed for the ego to develop and still hold the profound love relationship as a pair? Here again, it is a question of whether the unique elliptical dialogue can develop within the framework of the couple's relationship or whether it has to break because there are too many differences between them for their relationship to be sustainable.

When two become three, with the first child, the triangle is a challenge. In the mythological tale of Apuleius, as interpreted by Neumann (1956), Eros and Psyche name their child Joy. The interweaving of these two divine figures forms the *coniunctio*, the relational archetype, the fruit of which is their child Joy. This *coniunctio* takes place after the divine blessing from Aphrodite and Zeus and their individuation journeys, even though the emphasis is on Psyche's ego-self development. Eros also returns to his mother, Aphrodite, and frees himself from her control. We can learn from this mythological tale and see it as a collective script for the formation of a family and becoming relational.

In our daily lives, we struggle with these instincts and powers from our unconscious. How many of a baby's needs can we tolerate in our relationships? Here, the space needs to be redistributed between the ego, the pair and parenthood, where parenthood takes up most of the space and time available. The challenge in the elliptical dialogue is to enter into close relationship and at the same time hold and put our own needs to one side and confirm our partner in the adult relationship.

When children grow up, they have to follow their own paths with their unique repertoires of personality, gifts, and limits. Being a parent and a role model for the feminine and masculine is exciting and opens up for self-knowledge. The power in the child is enormous, in that you have to keep changing in order to keep the relationship with the child alive. This does not mean fulfilling every desire, but being warm and loving and attending to your own needs. In this life transformation of fathers, mothers, and adolescents, the exploration and crossing of borders and limits comes into focus. Sometimes these events can become necessary points for individuation and of becoming a more mature individual. It can also be dangerous and destructive. In the perspective of the elliptical dialogue, the energy- and libido-charged white area becomes visible, and in such a scenario it is important to be aware of how we react, both in terms of behaviour and words. The world outside the home becomes more and more integrated and understandable. Therefore, the dialogue with the world in different settings and how to assimilate the world gains focus. The use of language and words has to reflect contemporary culture and at the same time react to our own and our children's ego-self axes. The dialogue among parents, children and adolescents works if the language, ideas, and customs are combined with an understanding of the present situation or circumstances. There is a huge difference between asking, "Where have you been?" and getting the curt response "Out!" and formulating it in a way that encourages a more open and full response. The language and the dialogue need to be able to bridge the gap between the generations.

Creating your own unique place in the world takes time and is not always easy. When our offspring leave home to follow their own paths, we as parents will probably need to realign again as a couple. Will we look into each other's eyes and develop together, or is it an empty nest in which the dialogue is dead? Exploring and formulating this existential perspective can be difficult, and a new dialogue may need to be formulated. How will this new period of life be spent, and what will we want to do in the years that remain? The ego-self axis and the inner world become activated in a new modus. An awareness of life as limited and a sharper light on what kind of choices to make will be necessary. Being open to inner images, dreams, and urging voices will be helpful. Being able to tolerate the impact of the ego and the self in a fruitful dialogue with the self field and the archetypal fields that give new meaning for this new period with our partners is a challenge. The space in which parenthood took up most of the room can now be the place for renewal of a couple's life together and for our own individual development.

In the final life transition, we will again be alone. After the loss of loved ones, we have to come to terms with ourselves in one way or another. Will we be able to look back on life and accept what we have achieved or have not achieved. In one sense, this is a larger transformation than birth. At birth, we are received and held by the midwife and the mother. In the final transition, caring hands may soothe our skin and bodies, but no one knows what happens after death. Can we accept our mistakes and that we have damaged important relationships? Is there a way of gaining consciousness so that we can find peace and be more prepared for the end of our lives? The elliptical dialogue then goes into a perhaps more spiritual development, with a connection in the self-field to a spiritual space beyond and toward the unknown. Profound existential questions may arise. In some respect, the child's first question of "Who is going to take care of me?" is also the last existential question we might ask when passing the final threshold. "Who is going to take care of me?"

PART II
THE ELLIPTICAL DIALOGUE
AND TRANSFORMATION IN
JUNGIAN PSYCHOANALYSIS
– THE CLINICAL PART

5. Symbol as transformation

The elliptical dialogue and symbol in the red cylinder and black point, the ego-self axis. Clinical narrative.

From the blue frame described in the previous chapter as a general understanding, from mainly analytical psychology, of human existence as individuals and in relationships in the collective level, we will turn to specific clinical experience from Jungian psychoanalytical work. In this Part II, we will follow the twists and turns that unfold between myself and a patient, whom I name Björn. Clinical vignettes from analytical work with others will also be illustrated. I have had the privilege of meeting many different individuals and, as a result, being changed as an analyst and as a human being. Each of the chapters illustrates a perspective of analytical psychology and illuminates our mutual development. The three chapters—symbol, language, and active imagination as transformation—are connected to the map of the elliptical dialogue and, after presenting the clinical processes, are followed by theoretical analytical reflections. The analytical reflection following the clinical narrative weaves analytical psychology with relevant perspectives from systemic and language theory. Here, the intention is to look at the strong connecting threads.

The dog as a symbol of transformation will here illustrate the ego-self axis at work in the map of the elliptical dialogue. The red cylinder with the black point illustrates each individual's own ego-self axis.

We have already been introduced to Björn and know something about his situation. His family background can be summarized as follows. He was born into a wealthy family. His parents had settled in a more remote part of Sweden, where his father became the manager of the family company. His mother stayed at home and looked after Björn and his two brothers. During the Depression of the 1930s, the family company had to be sold, which naturally affected the self-image of Björn's father.

Both Björn's parents suppressed their artistic and creative skills. Björn talked about his father's violin never being played and his mother's passion for literature and intellectual discussions never being fully realized. In many ways, they were like strangers in the community and culture of farmers and workers. According to Björn, when his mother talked about her life situation, she stated, "I'm an orchid in this potato field!" Björn's paternal grandparents and their dogs also lived with the family, albeit in a house of their own.

The Rottweiler - Photo reprinted with permission from Björn.

From the previous life cycle model it is easy to imagine the crucial point when Björn was born as overwhelming and complex for the young couple. Björn was taken care of by a maid, whose caring and connecting ability later became important when he was neglected, abused, and thrown into the wardrobe.

As recounted in Part I, Björn entered my practice holding the Rottweiler dog image that he had painted from his powerful dream. Here it is on previous page 105:

From his family history, we can begin to reflect on how the dog, as a living symbol, became a companion in Björn's own life cycle. The dog forms a bridge from Björn's childhood to the analytical work, almost 70 years later. Here the dog enters the scene filled with an energy that longs to be transformed, translated, and embraced into consciousness.

Symbols and the Interpretation of Dreams is the title of an essay composed in English and completed shortly before Jung's death in June 1961. In this text, there is a section about the symbol's inherent power, called Healing the Split (CW 18 § 578 – 607). Here, Jung reflects on our loss of communication with nature:

> "This enormous loss is compensated by the symbols in our dreams. They bring up our original nature, its instincts and its peculiar thinking. Unfortunately, one would say, they also express their contents in the language of nature, which is strange and incomprehensible to us. It sets us the task of translating its images into the rational words and concepts of modern speech, which has liberated itself from its primitive encumbrances-notably from its mystical participation with things." (§ 586)

> "The words you use are empty and valueless, and they gain life and meaning only when you try to learn about their numinosity, their relationship to the living individual." (§ 590)

> "The symbol-producing function of our dreams is an attempt to bring our original mind back to consciousness, where it has never been before, and where it has never undergone critical self-reflection. We *have been* that mind, but we have never *known* it." (§ 591)

The analytical work as a whole can be seen as a weaving back and forth with a number of threads in the loom and one in the shuttle. When looking closer at the image of the dog, it seems somehow artificial. It is like pulling out a thread of the woven fabric and examining its way through the texture of Björn's life and our analytical work together. But for clarity, this is done here by recounting the clinical narrative from memory and the notes and images that Björn has agreed to include in the book. When I asked him what he thought about writing about our work together, he said: "If it is helpful to others, then I'll be happy to share, and now, with a calmer and more settled life situation, I might either be curious enough to read the text, or I might not be because now I'm occupied with more important perspectives. You know, I now talk with myself and others in a different way." It is in this moment that the elliptical dialogue transforms and becomes part of a united reality between us. The ego-self axis has developed so that the self aspect can go into the identity aspect as psyche and world as one, not divided or split as at the beginning of the ego-self development. From the beginning, a child's ego is embedded in self, and at the end of life this fuses again due to the ability of the psyche to live a symbolic life so that the self can appear as the centre of the ego. This development in the second half of life emanates from a stronger ego position that is able to connect and attach to the self in a way that unifies with the world.

IN THE DOGHOUSE

From the beginning, our relationship was tense. Björn stated very clearly from the start that he had lived with contradictions and tensions throughout his life. Now, this tension had become tangible in his dream about the Rottweiler and the Rottweiler saying, "If only you stand still, nothing will happen!" All the contradictions, tensions, highly energized manic states and depressive passive states were symbolized in the image of him holding the dog.

The dog is man's oldest domestic animal and a symbol of loyalty and faithfulness, but also of watchfulness and vigilance. In my thinking, it was as though the dog symbol had to lead the way and, in my own imagination, the image of walking a dog emerged. It stopped, examined, and sniffed at almost everything in its way. It was as though the dog was reading an exciting story. But it was also a Cerberus, the watchdog of Hades' realm, guarding territories and boundaries. Containing the dog image in my own imagination became important for amplifying and holding all the tensions and contradictions in Björn's actual life story. The dog symbol would lead us, show and tell us about the story of the symbol on our analytical journeying.

The first word that Björn tried to understand in depth was fearful. "It's a fearful position to hold, and how do we manage to live with such huge tensions, and why do they enter now?" It turned out that the experiences that were connected to that word enabled him to make contact with the feelings surrounding it during the therapy. Being able to put them into words by talking about the fearful situations he had encountered and being in dialogue with the symbol of the dog helped to ease the tensions. As a child, these dramatic, fearful, and violent situations were impossible for the psyche to comprehend. Björn, with his whole child being, was trapped inside this reality as an impossible reality for being. He was there, and the psyche had to protect itself. In Björn's case, this was done by dissociation. Björn's personality also prevented his psyche from being totally submerged. Such highly charged and abusive pain can easily lead to experiences of psychotic breakthrough. Björn's complex, rich inner life — and his ability to retract into his own inner world full of fantasy friends and play with his creative ability to make drawings and paintings — saved him from being totally fused and captured in constant affective arousal. But his personality became overwhelmed with affects and was unable to assimilate what was happening to him. The day after a punishment, everything was as usual, as though nothing special had happened.

Fear and horror seem to be emotions that in the first instance evoke dissociative reactions in traumatic situations. Rage, excitement, shame, and guilt are all part of a child's experience. The more contradictory the activated affects are, the harder it will be to assimilate an experience without dissociating from it. Bodily experiences that bring about dissociation are unbearably painful and bring confusing sexual arousal. Björn's experience as a small boy was of being pushed into the dark wardrobe by his father if he had been too enthusiastic about something. He may have shown his father a drawing that his father disliked and criticized. In the wardrobe, Björn could see the round white light of the moon shining through a small window. Sometimes, one of the maids would come and open the door slightly, whispering, "How are you, Björn?"

When talking about these experiences of built-up tension, explosion, and discharge, he was also able to connect with his early childhood memories of safety and peace of mind. These memories reminded him how, with his grandmother's permission, he would sneak into the doghouse and spend time with the dogs. These moments were profoundly comforting and trusting. His body and soul connected to the warmth of the dogs, and he was able to participate in the mysterious exchange between himself and the animal world. During analysis, he described the conversations between him and the dogs in which he was resting his head on the dogs' bellies, listening to their breathing, and it became clear that the symbol was one of love, trust, and joy.

Using language and narrative perspectives in this kind of symbolic work helps to create a new, more coherent and less dissociated and split image of the dog. The memory of Björn lying beside the dogs in the doghouse came to life when he asked himself the question: *Was I ever enclosed by caring and connection in security and freed from fear?* I responded, "Let's stay with your question" and then repeated it, adding, "Let's breathe together for a while and see what comes to mind. An image or language." In this silent space with closed eyes and mutual breathing, his psyche was able to stay with the image of him lying with the dogs. Looking and describing this image from different perspectives, yet still holding onto the basic question of care posed by Björn, allowed these five perspectives to emerge:

- Exploring the concept of care and connection, from the present perspective via words and breathing.

- Seeing and describing in words the child Björn with the dogs in the doghouse.

- From the adult perspective of imagining having a conversation with the dogs.

- in the fourth perspective, in the green elliptical dialogue, being able to tentatively formulate Björn's experience of deep connection.

- Finally, being able to reflect on the existential question of caring and connection from a consciousness that is deeply connected with self-images promotes a more coherent development of the ego-self axis.

In all these five perspectives a number of ego-self relations are at work. In my own ego-self axis, I have the image of a spiral staircase. These five different perspectives form a number of inner ego-self relations and lead to different ego-self intrapsychic dialogues. In the green elliptical interpersonal dialogue between Björn and myself, I became sensitive to where Björn might be in his inner ego-self relationship, which enabled me, as his analyst, to accept his invitation to dialogue.

In the first perspective, I used the rhythm of breathing to develop our energies and resilience. Sitting opposite each other, breathing naturally and rhythmically and allowing our body language to emerge was a conscious choice. Here, the green ellipse held our different individual ego-self axes. We were in what can be described as the archaeological field of language, feelings, and affects. A gestural language. If we are careful and cautious, we can discover new connections in this field in the form of dialogical words and body positions relating to our ongoing analytical work. The question Björn asked at the beginning of one of our sessions was answered by new painful discoveries.

Memories of violence and rejection surfaced. His ego-self axis would sometimes break out in the session, and I was conscious of guarding the Cerberus position of the blue frame in the elliptical dialogue. Toward the end of each session I would say, "Now we have 10 minutes left in which to close and connect. We have done deep work, and you now need to be aware of your steps and balance when going home." He would respond by saying, "I will try to leave the fearful images of my Rottweiler here when I step over the threshold to outer life." He shook my hand and left. This *rite of passage* became part of the language we developed together. My own ego-self axis was centred on maintaining a position in which I could both acknowledge his pain and confirm our relationship as a collaboration in an interlinked work.

In the second perspective, when in his inner images Björn was in the doghouse feeling the warmth of the dogs' bellies and sleeping with them like a puppy, his language changed. His voice lowered, and his narrative assumed the "I" perspective. "I'm lying on the dogs' bellies and feeling their breath on my chin. I can smell a mixture of moist warmth and soil from their coats. I fall asleep." These new discoveries emerged with new perspectives on his and my ego-self's inner relationship. For example, when calibrating our mutual breath, it was a result of how we as human beings calibrate ourselves to each other. The discovery of the mirror neurons (Bauer 2007) is a neurobiological aspect of this phenomena. Imagining a walk with another person is another well-known human experience. After only a few minutes, the length of your respective steps will adjust to a mutual rhythmical movement enclosed with a turn taking in words, listening, and reflecting, all in the package of the elliptical dialogue. We human beings do this instinctively if we listen to the rhythm of life and health. With Gadamer (2003) in mind, it is the three rhythmical phenomena of breathing, metabolization, and sleep that form this unbroken course of events in us and promotes life, energetic processes, and resilience. Thus, the dog symbol combined with breathing became important for archetypal images from the self-field to emerge. In images of body and breathing, the little boy Björn and the dogs became a coherently told experience. By this time, during analysis, it became clear that the Rottweiler in him held the tensions of polarities and opposites and that Björn was aware that this kind of dog demanded respect. But when Björn's Rottweiler said, "If you only stand still, nothing would happen!" I thought of it as standing still, not stiffening, but slowing down in a conscious yet still way—like a slow examination of the two images of *The Rottweiler* and *In the Doghouse*. When these two dog images were constellated, it was also possible for Björn to imagine a conversation taking place—first as a fantasy conversation, with the dogs in the doghouse, and in between hours as an active imagination with the

Rottweiler. Images from the active imagination are here below presented as illustrations *Rottweiler - Bear building a blue house* (p. 112) and as *Oh, I'm so tired of standing!* (p. 114) But the first dialogical imagination was with the dogs in the doghouse in one of our sessions.

The third perspective then unfolded, namely Björn having an imaginary conversation, as an adult, with the dogs in the doghouse. The settlement of the adult perspective as a starting point is important, because it means that in the session the ego has its gaze pointed to the previous constellated image of the doghouse. In my view, it is important to let the inner image of a memory of security come into being before deeply deconstructing traumatic experiences in therapy. This does not mean that the experiences and their impact they have should be denied. On the contrary. However, it is important to create an inner blue frame together with more clearly developed ego-self axis and connect this to the image so that the setting as a whole is safe and secure. It is interesting that the dialogue between Björn and the dog unfolded as a fantasised dialogue in a session when Björn saw himself lying with the dogs in a sleepy state. In this dialogue, Björn says, "I'm here again," and the dog responds by saying: "Hmm, I can smell you, come here and rest." The image is already known and connected to dialogue and breathing. We can easily imagine Björn's gestures and body posture when the tensions were released. This image, connected to the exchange of an archetypal symbolic dialogue of trust and security, became our unique and clearing language. This image made it possible to create a dialogical network and explore the experiences of disconnection and abusiveness in deep ways. This ability of the psyche to constellate polarities from inner images develops from inner undifferentiated, pleromatic areas toward creatura, and then it begins to differentiate within the blue frame of the analytic experience. For Björn, this differentiation was facilitated by my reflection at the end of the first hour of analysis: "I wonder whether this room and our meetings could be a place in which you, me and your Rottweiler feel comfortable?" After moments of silence he answered: "I will consider this, but anyway the dog has to stay here, and I'll be back next week." We then shook hands, and he left. He came back the following week.

At the beginning of our time together he would sit at the edge of his chair, lean forward, and be eager to tell his stories. When the pain, ease, and comfort emerged in our dialogue, sometimes accompanied by tears, his body relaxed a little, and he could lean backward and be less tense.

The fourth perspective of the development of the ego-self axis comes when words and dialogue begin to produce new connections of consciousness. This has to do with the strengthening of the ego position, an ego position that

Rottweiler – Bear building a blue house
Photo reprinted with permission from Björn

is in deep contact with the self-field and is able to create archetypal symbolic images. During our analytical process, Björn kept company with the Rottweiler in between sessions. One day he showed me this image:

This image came after a break for the summer holidays. The four-week separation was difficult for Björn to deal with. However, with this image he was able to express a longing for the continuation of our work for the first time. He had been in active imaginative company with the Rottweiler, which had decided to build himself a new house. In this mutual field of active imagination, there had been a development of the dog's own individuation process. The self-image emerged as part dog and part human. I saw this illustration as a language for increased and strengthened ego-self ability and for his inner creative work during our break.

We continued, and I deliberately tuned into Björn's breathing in every session in order to get a sense of the pressure he was under when working with his early childhood traumatic experiences. This enabled me to be vigilant about respecting his integrity. Breathing and movements of the body are interwoven.

The ongoing breathing cycle, from inhalation to exhalation to inhalation and so on, is coherent with the corresponding movements of the muscles in the body, even if the eye does not register this. In other words, the inhaled air "goes" right to the body's extremities of fingertips and toes. For various reasons, the muscles become tense, which prevents the air from moving freely. In other instances, the entire chest becomes tense, thus preventing the flow of air. This happens when, for one reason or another, the expressions of body and words are suppressed.

Sometimes a person experiences that the circumstances do not welcome expression. One way of preventing such expression is to restrict one's breathing. For Björn, this became evident when his memories of restraint and violence in childhood were reawakened and also when he was eager to produce what was expected in the analytical relationship. His imagination of how I should present myself and be available for him in the hour and between the hours was attached to an image of me that was highly idealized and instructional. When he was in that image, he was so restricted that he was unable to listen and be free. Reaching some kind of relaxed tension in the analytical relationship was a struggle for us both. As I understood it, his imaginative capacity was highly restricted by fear and the fearful position of holding the Rottweiler. For a lot of our time together, Björn was afraid to plumb the depths of his pain, which was why the transference was so filled with his need for control and erotic fantasies. I had to be very clear with him and confront the boundaries when he tried to intimidate me by making suggestions of an erotic nature and getting too close physically. I regarded these experiences as necessary to develop the analysis and understood it as the highly charged erotic transference stood in the way of his individuation and, one can also say, in the way of the whole analysis to individuate. I became both strict and firm and described when and how he passed my limits. Not an easy task, but the inner image of the red cylinder and black point as one ego-self axis of my own and of his building and forming of his ego-self as symbolized in the *Rottweiler - Bear building a blue house* helped me. It increased my ambiguity tolerance and had my empathy directed toward the individuation process of the beginning of Bjorn's ego-self development.

To refer to the map of the elliptical dialogue, for both Björn and myself, most of the activity in this phase of the analysis took place in the blue frame and the ego-self positions. The recounting of his childhood experiences occurred on the green elliptical line of the dialogue, while I adopted a listening and supportive position, asked clarifying questions, acknowledged his pain, and normalized his childish behaviour when he felt too much shame. But in that phase, listening and responding to my words was hard for him. It was as though he sat at the edge of the chair ready to fire off his story. Gradually, the story of his childhood could be linked to his experiences as an adult, to his relationship with his three wives and four children, to his fear of feelings, to the terror he felt inside when the man in his mind appeared and lowered the curtain to make everything black. It could also be linked to the statements he made about ending the analysis because he considered himself to have been thoroughly analyzed and did not need more. But gradually the memories emerged and with them images of childhood connected to pain, violence, and suffering. Sometimes, the Rottweiler and its fearful position were mentioned during the work with his mother and father complexes. I was aware of this in my ego position, just as I was also aware of Börn's limited capacity to reach the self-field. However, when we did reach this space, after a lot of mutual work, the air became much freer for us both. This occurred when he was able to talk about his grandparents' dogs and when his mother and father complex was not so highly charged.

The fifth perspective of being be able to reflect on the existential question of caring and connection from a consciousness that is in deep connection with

'Oh, I'm so tired of standing!' - Photo reprinted with permission from Björn

self-images promoted by a more coherent ego-self axis development, was facilitated by the following image:

Björn told me the dialogue between himself and the Rottweiler:

"'Now I must stand on my four feet, that's my natural position,'" the dog stated. "So I let him down, and what a relief that was for both of us. Then I could stand on my two legs as a human being," Björn said as he handed over the drawing. I said, "I can see you are both separate but united at the bottom of the drawing. And you are looking both forward and facing me when I look at the image."

Was I ever enclosed by caring and connection in security and free from fear? This was a burning question throughout the analytical work. Although we searched for possible perspectives and reflections, we never ended up with one simple answer. However, in this fifth perspective, it was possible to express several ego perspectives in language. This was made possible by the fact that the self-field and the archetypal field of the image of the dog was connected to the ego position at the same time and at the time of dialogue.

During this period of the analysis, the theme of being close and separate began to emerge at different levels. "What does the distance between myself and others look like? What can I do in this distance—how can I be there?" Questions like this began to emerge for Björn. The image also came after a three-week summer break. During this intermission, he missed our work a lot and, as a parallel discourse, began to paint goddesses with birds' heads modeled from cave paintings in the Sahara Desert considered to be some 5,000 years old. I received the two images at the same time and thanked him for them. In the sessions that followed, we worked on closeness, intimacy, and separateness, being alone and being together. We used Björn's narratives about his marriages and his professional position, how his temper and sensitivity were both a benefit and a curse, and how he found it difficult to create a free zone around his work as a journalist with deadlines and doing his own artwork.

I began to see the archetypally charged self-field that had first presented itself as the standing togetherness of himself and the dog change and observed the beginning of an ego-self that could connect with his inner relationships. Having said this, Björn still remained dependent on our archetypal transference relationship, which was symbolized as goddesses with birds' heads. So was I, because this formed one of the basic archetypal symbols of our relationship. This was both a parallel and an interconnected movement in our work. As a conclusion from the three Rottweiler illustrations, words and dialogue became a part of the development of the dog symbol. When this was made room for in our analytic sessions, the ability for Björn to be in a dialogic way with me increased. *It was as if the dogs' ability with words and language led Bjorn to more of a listening and reflecting position in our relationship.*

SYMBOL AND LANGUAGE AS EMBODIED CONSCIOUSNESS

C. G. Jung and Ludwig Wittgenstein can help to clarify what happened between Björn and myself when following the symbol of the dog. People coming to therapy with emotional problems often do a lot of what is known as gesture talk. The pain itself is often manifested as gesture talk, which is a sublingual vocabulary that brings us to the point of what the analysis is trying to address. John Shotter (2008) is an innovative social thinker whose writings on the nature of dialogical communication have become relevant to relational therapies. He creates an intellectual pool around the ideas of the Russian literature scientist Mikhail Bachtin (1895-1975) and Ludwig Wittgenstein. For my part, I like to think of gesture talk as a hidden realm.

Wittgenstein explains also that by "primitive," he means that this sort of behaviour is prelinguistic: that a language is based on it, that it is the prototype of a way of thinking and not the result of thought. In this respect, Wittgenstein's intimations are similar to those of Bateson and Jung. Here, I am thinking of Jung's images of the self that present themselves in the form of symbols in dreams and in our bodies as reactions and gestures.

Bateson regarded the sublingual form of relational dialogues as "syllogisms in metaphor." Bateson had a lifelong interest in the kinds of sublingual communication that are common to religion, humour, playfulness, some forms of madness, animal communication and art, and put together "the beginnings of a creatural grammar" (Bateson & Bateson, 1987.) Bateson used Jung's term "creatura" to describe the world of the living, as opposed to the "pleroma." The pleroma has no mental processes, names, or classes. The creatura, on the other hand, is based on patterns and communicates through language, using similes and metaphors in a variety of embedded and embodied ways. When it come to the concept of "language game," Wittgenstein intends to highlight that "the talking of language is a part of an activity and form for life" (Wittgenstein 1953/1992 § 23 p. 21). This focus brings Jung, Wittgenstein, and Bateson together and forms a common entrance into the map of the elliptical dialogue. Here, the three theories meet in a fruitful possibility for the development of a perspective for thinking about what goes on in a meeting of minds, such as that we experience when doing, acting, and being in psychotherapy.

PART II
THE ELLIPTICAL DIALOGUE
AND TRANSFORMATION IN
JUNGIAN PSYCHOANALYSIS
– THE CLINICAL PART

6. Language as transformation

The elliptical dialogue and language in the green elliptical line. Clinical narrative.

In Björn's life, the law was connected to the word, and the word came from the father. "In my inner world, the words went deep inside myself. My father's words, when I was a child (…).

"And this was given, the world as my father had told it. And at the same time it was different. Something more, something else, and something that was not told. Something that was true, also. But no one said that. It was in a place of its own, outside. Outside the circle of light around our dining table. Maybe within the wardrobe. This world could not be spoken. It was as though it was nonexistent. But it existed, was present. Only it was not possible to tell, not possible to think, it had no word. It was not allowed to have words. Because the words were the reality, and there was no room for creating anything else. Outside the circle of light was, death. These other words, they were death. They were nothing, blank, black."

This reflection emerged in a session of retrospect and consolidation and the weaving together of words and images from our work with the father complex. I was able to offer my reflection on the green elliptical line: "But Björn, what kind of words were the unpermitted words?" Björn said: "What comes to my mind now are just words for obstinacy: No. Will not. They could not be spoken, because from these words represented devastation, denial, and commitment of sin."

"Is it the word from the father that forbids?" I asked. "Yes, but it is also the sought-for gaze from the father that permits. It is as if the whole being came and stemmed from these eyes and made me want to be warm. Outside this is death. As there is obstinacy and denial, the words 'will not' are very dangerous because then I was in exile. My ego and I became connected to the outside in the blank and the black."

This dialogue took place a few years into our analytical work. In a reflective session of retrospect when having the following three illustrations of the father complex placed on the carpet in front of us. I think that this dialogue was able to emerge due to the mutual experience and trust that Björn and I had developed whilst working with his images and the various interactions between us, which included connection, painful ruptures, and reconnection.

Now following is a presentation from three illustrations of seeing into image and words inside and behind, below and beyond the father complex.

"THY WILL BE DONE!"

In many respects, our work with the father complex was fascinating. Right from the beginning the word "fearful" was connected to the first image of the Rottweiler. In the exploration of this word, Björn talked about his childhood and the importance of the dog as a symbol of fear and warmth. This is an underlying holding structure. The complexity and polarity of the self symbol that was held and contained by and in our relationship allowed the symbol to develop to its full potential, with the self to emerge. This work created a containing foundation for a further inner restructuring and decharging of the father complex.

I would like to invite you to enter a breathing space. Take a moment to reflect on the following three images of the father complex.

First Silence - Photo reprinted with permission from Björn

Father Murder or a Fairy Tale Just a Fairy Tale - Photo reprinted with permission from Björn

Divided but One - **Photo reprinted with permission from Björn**

Björn sees his father in front of him, who is going to torment him with his whip. At the end of the whip, there is a swastika, although Björn is not primarily afraid of the forthcoming pain. "It is the images. What I will see in them. The seeing in itself is the most horrible." He continues to talk while I listen and look into his eyes. "You see this seeing, this sight, the horror, is on one side humiliation but also the more general recognition of the repetition, the recurrence." He continues: "I'm also afraid of his blank face. What would it be like if he became more visible? I'm thinking that he is totally devastated in his face. Red, open flesh wound. No face anymore, I am afraid of him and the appearance of that sight. Therefore, the blank quadrangular form in the image."

Björn sits close to me. His gaze wanders and rests on the carpet in the room. I tell him, slowly, that I have listened to his words. He then recounts a memory from just before his father's death: "I remember he asked, just before I was about to leave him in the hallway, if I thought he had been too hard with us children, with my brothers and myself." I said just one word: 'Yes.' My father became silent, and for a moment perhaps I could see his eyes. Maybe this moment was a kind of confirmation that he had been thinking about his tyranny. Maybe a glimpse of his eyes seeing with my eyes."

When he leaves the therapy session, I hold out my hand. We stand there for a little longer than usual and our eyes meet.

At a meta-level, Björn's reflections on the concept of the blank, blinding, dazzling, and daring face connect to Jung's writings about the symbol. It is also easy to refer to the image of God as a face that is not visible but that provokes reactions of blinding, fear, devotion, surrender, and worship. In Björn's life, the archetypal symbol of the father and his actual father were interwoven. Later in the analysis, when the father complex had become more conscious and discharged, the libido in the father archetype was set free to develop and explore his Christian faith. The self and its inherent capacity for libido became a way of experiencing the inner room for spirituality. For Björn, this development involved breaking away from a fundamentalist Christian movement to become freer in his reflecting and searching for how spirituality might be more meaningful for him in his own personal life.

This bridge from personal to spiritual work is possible in analytical psychology. In *Minding the Self: Jungian Meditations on Contemporary Spirituality*, Murray Stein (2014) addresses this by stating that: "The purpose of analysis is to convert symbols into signs and metaphors and so to free the patient's consciousness from the grip of the unconscious complexes and to unblock the flow of libido into more satisfying channels of living, loving, and creating. This opens the way of fuller incarnation of the self in a person's life" (Stein 2014 p. 30).

BUT FIRST FALLING

Björn called the second image *Father Murder or a Fairy Tale Just a Fairy Tale*. This marked a crucial development in his analytical journey in terms of building the ego-self axis. It also marked a crucial point in our interpersonal relationship concerning the green elliptical line of dialogue and its possibilities and boundaries. Further, it marked a crucial point of development in the Hermes area of libido, with regard to its uncontrollable, explosive, and surprising nature.

Obstinacy, denial, defiance, and the words "I will not" were dangerous because they connected the I, or ego, to the outside surroundings. Uttering these words meant taking the risk of being banned and becoming an outlaw. However, as the drive for individuation was strong, Björn said that "living in the father country was impossible and a dilemma. This country made itself comfortable in myself at the same time as I have become a stranger in this inner country. I cannot live there, but it lives inside myself as an inner position." Much later, when he was able to reflect on the analytical process as a whole, and especially on that particular experience, he said, "That experience, when it happened, was really dangerous."

WHAT HAPPENED?

When Björn entered with the image of *Father murder*, it was similar to his entrance with *The Rottweiler* in the sense that he was extremely excited, but also different because by then we had done a lot of work together on containing and unfolding his experience of growing up with his parents and brothers. As always, at this stage the analytical relationship serves the purpose of making the analysand feel contained and safe symbolically and supported by a good mother. Being understood, confirmed, and, in the elliptical dialogue, reaching the experience of being able to put together a fairly emotionally coherent story of your life as a child forms the basis for further development and individuation. But this stage of being dominated by maternal energy cannot last and at some point the analytical relationship has to change. I think that this change manifests itself and develops from both the analysand's and the analyst's self-fields. It manifests itself via archetypal and symbolic images and movements that are specific to this unique analytical journey. This can be likened to paternal energy entering that of the mother and child. This entrance of masculine energy means a break for the psyche when something enters from the outside.

In our work, this shift entered like a surprise and became a dangerous rupture. Holding the image in his hands when entering, Björn boldly stated: "Before we start, you must take a look at this; now, here, take it and, come on, give me big hug! Don't you think I've been a clever boy?" I felt overwhelmed by his eager emotional reaction. Physically, I pulled back and created a distance between us. He expected a more joyful, confirming reaction than I was capable of providing. He instinctively noticed my cool response, which for him meant rejection, refusal, and punishment at a deeper level. I became the punishing father who flung him into the wardrobe. I knew in my rational mind and felt that he was in a vulnerable stage of our analytical work in terms of the development of his creativity; a creativity that his father punished both physically and psychologically. Björn's ego was also growing and coming more into consciousness. In the image, the archetypal archer boy shoots his arrow at the monstrous father. The arrow forms a strong vector, pointing diagonally over the void toward the scary father silhouette. It is like seeing someone flex the bow like Ulysses to put an end to the ruthless exploitation of the suitors. Symbolically, Björn was in charge of his bow, able to fire an arrow and put an end to the inner father exploitive destructiveness that did not allow his ego function to develop. This image in itself formed a turning point in terms of a suitably equipped ego archer.

Complex dynamic forces are at work in this brief but precious moment when the Father Murder image emerged. I was aware of Björn's pain and rage toward his father, who constantly devalued and despised him. However, in this moment I also became the punishing father, in that I fused with the father complex. Did I destroy this important numinous experience, or was it something that would be possible to work through in our ongoing elliptical dialogue? At that particular moment knowing was impossible. It really depended on the stability of Björn's inner image of our relationship and whether he could hold a memory of a symbolically holding mother that could cope with a little boy's rage. It also ultimately depended on my position as a person and an analyst. I felt very awkward and uncomfortable about my rejection of him and the fact that I had immediately pulled back. Such an act would be difficult to erase.

INHABITING MYSELF

Language and mutual dialogue are based on telling, listening, and reflection. As I saw it, Björn's and my ego-self axes were in different positions in the map of the elliptical dialogue. Björn behaved like a little boy eager for confirmation. His ego was at that moment not capable of judging the situation from a more mature perspective of not overwhelming his analyst with demands for kisses and hugs. The instinctive behaviour of my ego-self axis was to draw back, because I did not want to be kissed and hugged. Here, Björn broke my physical and psychological integrity. Our respective inner ego-self relationships were in two different places and could not be held by the green elliptical line of dialogue. There are limits for the possibility of dialogue, and we had reached one of them.

The sessions that followed this rupture were intense and accompanied by rage, hard words, and rapid breathing. I tried to follow his rhythm without losing my own. I used breathing as a metaphor so that I could follow Björn's speed and shifts by listening, thinking, and talking. Many of his sentences began with "I," as though he made himself at home in his self in the sense of inhabiting a space that was his own and did not belong to his father. He individuated with words, sounds, and gestures. He put his painful experience into words and acted it out. He accused me of being cold and too much of an analytical fundamentalist, which I found difficult to deal with without becoming defensive. I remember that during this period we had some intense experiences together when he talked to me as though I was his father. He used the words of a little boy. I tried my best to listen, but it was hard because I thought he was being much too unfair. At the end of such a session, I asked him for how he felt inside, and he answered: "I feel fine, and thank you for being here with me, listening." I remember being surprised but gradually learned to be utterly attentive in an active listening position.

Now, reflecting from a meta-level, I think that this position both restored and kept our green elliptical line intact, albeit silently. There was capacity for resilience within us both. From the perspective of our respective ego-self axes, the transcendent function was fully active. I had the responsibility of keeping a balance in the elliptical dialogue so that the relationship between our respective ego-self axes could develop.

I would also like to say something about how I understood what happened between us with the aid of systemic thinking and Gregory Bateson's ideas about differences that make differences. Bateson brought to our attention that we do not see things as things in themselves, but as something different that is not separated from its background. We "picture" a man as something distinct from his background. The picture contains both background and man. Man himself sees and describes his background in terms of the differences he sees. He will be acquainted or familiar with his background in terms of the differences he can see, hear, smell, touch, and taste. Bateson defines something that is different from the surroundings as "the making of a distinction." Many distinctions can be made. Think of all distinctions one sense can make and then contemplate what five senses can do! Reflect also on what two people with five senses can do in an analytical dialogue. Then, contemplate on what happened in my dialogue with Björn when The Father Murder image emerged and Björn was thrown back to the days when he was 8 years of age. I think I saw both the 8-year-old boy and the elderly man at the same time. But these distinctions were too different, and we had two very different "maps" of the same "territory", as Bateson would have put it. What happened was that our elliptical dialogue had a rupture in it. In other words, there is always more to see than one sees. There is no one correct history, one correct picture, or one correct "different map" of the "territory." This was my challenge when Björn confronted my cold response and spoke to me as though I was his father. Bateson's ideas make me want to know more. What did the other person see, smell, hear, or feel that I was not aware of in the situation? These new aspects of the moving "picture" can stimulate differences in my own evolving "picture." Bateson's famous sentence, "The elementary unit of information is a difference that makes a difference," is important here. The verb "to make" suggests that the difference that is made, is made by a difference over time. Bateson says a difference over time is a change. In short, there are two different meanings in Bateson's use of the word difference: that something is distinct in that it is different from its background; and that a change is a difference over time brought about by a difference.

I think that these ideas form an important basis for clinical analytical work in terms of how we use words (come into being) in the elliptical dialogue. What would happen if instead of the word "difference," we used the more everyday word "unusual." If people are exposed to the usual, they tend to stay the same, whereas if they encounter something that is unusual, it might induce change. If the new that they meet is very (too) unusual, they close up in order to keep and conserve their integrity. Therefore, what we as analysts should strive for is to provide something that is unusual but not too unusual in the ongoing elliptical dialogue. This includes the setting and frame in which we meet, the themes or issues the elliptical dialogue covers, and the form it takes.

By remaining attentive to Björn's words about how he had experienced his father, and as if I was his father, I was able to ask him at the end of each such session what he was feeling at that precise moment. When he answered, "Good, and thank you for listening," I understood in my own inner dialogue that we were engaged in an unusual but not too unusual elliptical dialogue. The archetypal archer boy in the second image fires his arrow at the monstrous father silhouette across a void. It can be seen as a sublimation of a psychic content of strong energy with a vector quality in the powerful symbolic image. It is really a way of loosening the ego defences and becoming more tolerant of and integrating with the whole ego position. If the ego-self axis is broken in the tyranny of the fatherland, where a split-off part of the "I" is in exile and unable to exist, this image indicates very strongly that a healing of the split in the ego-self axis is taking place. At the very same moment that Björn offered me his image, the green elliptical line broke. How might this moment be understood? Could it also be seen as a necessary enactment of the split ego-self axis and a moment that was given to us so that our self planes could be restored? My analytical understanding of this is that the psyche allowed integration to happen. Imagine what would have happened if I'd said: "Oh, what a powerful image, Björn!" He might have kissed and hugged me, and I might have let it happen and inside myself said, "Let it be." There may have been a little ethical growling sound of awkwardness in a corner of my analytical persona. I might have rationalized: "But never mind! And besides, this mutual hug is important for Björn in his vulnerable state of growth."

This moment is the intermediate state of liminality. In the image and in the room of my practice between Björn and myself, the archer boy as a child archetype is in the company of an 8-year-old boy who wants to be embraced and acknowledged by me as an analyst and the person I am. We are at different levels in our respective ego-self axes and in different positions in the domain of the blue frame. There is a break in the green elliptical line of the dialogue that is captured by the white Hermes energetic area of the trickster and of unbridled and untamed energy.

The child archetype is one of the most powerful. Jung writes the following in his essay, "The Psychology of the Child Archetype": "Not for a moment dare we succumb to the illusion that an archetype can be finally explained and disposed of. Even the best attempts at explanation are only more or less successful translations into another metaphorical language. (Indeed, language itself is only an image.) The most we can do is to *dream the myth onwards* and give it a modern dress. And whatever explanation and interpretation does to it, we do to our own souls as well, with corresponding results for our own well-being. The archetype—let us never forget this—is a psychic organ present in all of us" (Jung 1940/1969: § 271).

Did we dream the myth onward? Did we give it a modern dress on our analytical six-year journey? There is no given answer to this, but let us follow the theme of language as transformation and stay with the third image, which Björn called *Divided but One*.

In retrospect, when these three images were laid out on the carpet in my room, Björn was at the end of analytical work. He was engaged in a dialogue about leaving and being left out. He was also engaged in the most intense living of his own life, had again experienced the love of a woman, and was prepared to continue to develop and grow. By then, the elliptical dialogue had become both a symbol and a transformer for how to make libido flow in a way that was not blocked by complexes. It was also on its way to becoming internalized in us. In my professional individuation as a Jungian psychoanalyst, I reflected on how this work had changed my own ego-self axis development in the second half of life. I also began to realize that writing about the experience might enable me to process it internally and perhaps share it with others. It dawned on me that it could also be of interest for others in the same professional field.

When I asked Björn what had happened to him in our analytical work, he told me that the image *Divided but One* was an image of his own inner state: "On the one hand, it can be seen as a very exhilarated part of myself trying to walk away from the depressed side of myself. And yes I know I had to have breaks in our work. And every time I came back, it was good and painful to see you again. But you were also so uploaded with intense erotic sensations that I almost could not bear the tension. The breaks were also very much about having to leave you as my symbolic father and as my symbolic mother." He continued: "But now with this image and the three images lying in front of us on your carpet, I am more conscious of how the swing flows within, from one side to another. I am … I am able to say 'I' without judging the 'I' as something hollow. It is though it has to sink before it is allowed to be spoken. The day has come now, more and more, when I can say 'I' without reflecting on it, without this being a question of my total right of existence, but as making myself present with my whole being, then I am…"

In terms of ego-self axis development, this can be understood as the growth of a coherent ego-self axis that is in contact with self-field, which is further developed on the archetypal field in order to contain the ego in the transcendent energy of the ego-self axis. The ego split that Björn talked about at the beginning, when the Father was the Law and "No. Will not" was in exile, had become an Outlaw. The ego defenses of the child Björn, erected as a way of enduring his father's tyranny, were a necessary part of this development. The ego defenses then loosened up because they were no longer needed, and the "I" no longer needed to be split off. This resulted in a tolerance of the existence of the wholeness of the ego-self axis in flow. The ego matured, and the whole ego-self relationship in the psyche individuated and tolerated the impact of the mature ego. This meant that the symbol of the Outlaw could be discharged.

The work with the ruptures was difficult. I was able to address the reunion during the break. Björn never walked out of a session but stated that on a couple of occasions he felt himself to have been "thoroughly analysed" and did not need any more sessions. But he returned, and we continued. In this sense, there was a swing in the rhythm and sometimes ruptures in the weekly sessions. I always kept his weekly time free during the breaks that he initiated. It was also difficult to take his criticism of me as being too impersonal. This occurred more frequently when, as I saw it, his ego-self axis was fused and he acted like a little baby.

From his intellectual position, Björn was often sharply critical and, as he developed a more oedipal state in his ego-self growth, the erotic charge in our dialogue became increasingly obvious. He commented on how I dressed, on what suited me, and would often scrutinize me as he came into my practice and presented me with sensual drawings. I must have shown embarrassment, because he would immediately notice this and asked if it was the case. Switching on to our analytical work was often difficult as a result. But part of me was also flattered and gave me an opportunity to reflect on my own feminine traits. A challenging but deep experience of this whole analytical work was that Björn was always in his true authentic state. He never put on a mask or adjust to what he thought I expected from him. He never came across as unauthentic. The image *Divided but One* can also be seen as a symbolic image of our work, including its ruptures. The image showed both an excited and a depressed Björn, which he regarded as reflecting his true state: "I am a mixture of both." I also see it as an illustration of the archetypal analytical movements ongoing in the elliptical dialogue. One differentiating separatio movement and one synthesising coniunctio movement.

PART II
THE ELLIPTICAL DIALOGUE
AND TRANSFORMATION IN
JUNGIAN PSYCHOANALYSIS
– THE CLINICAL PART

7. Active imagination as transformation

The elliptical dialogue and active imagination in the white energized field of Hermes. Clinical narratives.

In 1916, Jung wrote a paper called "The transcendent function" (Jung C W 8 1916/1957/1981). Interestingly, this paper remained in Jung's files until 1953, when it was discovered by students at the C. G. Jung Institute. First published in 1957, in the preface Jung writes about active imagination: "The method of 'active imagination,' hereinafter described, is the most important auxiliary for the production of those contents of the unconscious which lie, as it were, immediately below the threshold of consciousness and, when intensified, are the most likely to irrupt spontaneously into the conscious mind."

Active imagination is one of the cornerstones of analytical psychology, and many psychoanalysts and scholars have developed this concept further (Joy Shaverein in JAP, 2007, 52, 413-431, Sherry Salman in ed Stein 2010). For me, the concept has its roots in Jung's philosophical grounding in alchemy and his experiences as outlined in The Red Book (2009). I can see many similarities to meditation and other expressive art therapies, although there is one basic difference. Active imagination always starts from the given inner images, i.e., the images that are given by the psyche from within. Active imagination never proposes or sets a scene. From the analyst's point of view, you follow and receive the given images.

In the following three vignettes, I present my understanding of how to work with active imagination. First, there are two scenes from Joanna and Helen. Then, in the third vignette, we revisit Björn's symbol of the dog and continue to follow its individuation process. In all three clinical examples analytical psychology is interwoven with language theory and systems theory.

THE FROG VOICE MONSTER

This clinical narrative is from a work done together with Joanna, and I want to share how active imagination can be a help on different levels. We have worked together for many years, and one day I received this email from her:

"Innan jag började hos dig så kändes det som om jag höll på att försvinna, att det inte fanns någon plats där jag kunde vara jag. Men jag sökte ju hjälp. Jag visste inte var det skulle innebära, men sökte ändå hjälp.

Och det var först när jag fick kontakt med dig som det var möjligt för mig att gå hela vägen ner och tillbaka, att våga känna och prata om den där svarta tomheten. Och även om jag har utvecklats under den tid som vi har haft kontakt, för det känner jag ju att jag har gjort, så behöver jag vara uppmärksam på signaler när det börjar bära iväg åt något håll.

Det var bara det jag ville skriva."

"Before I started seeing you, I felt as though I was about to disappear, that there was no place in which I could be myself. But I sought help. I did not know then what that would mean, but I anyway sought help.

It was only when I contacted you that it became possible for me to go all the whole way down and back and dare to feel and talk about the black emptiness. And even though I have grown and developed during the time we have had contact, because I really feel that I have, I still need to be aware of signals when things start to move in another direction.

I just wanted you to know."

The following question came to mind: What is the crucial experience in analysis that creates a bow that is strong enough to carry life on?

Joanna had a black, tearing hole in her stomach. The tearing force threatened her existence. When we started to work together, this strong power emerged as an inner creature. In one of our sessions she told me: "In many fairy tales there is a story about the princess that kisses a frog—and suddenly, there is a prince! But that's not my story." I reflected on the fairy tale about the frog prince, when the princess's golden ball is lost in the pond and the frog says, "You'll get it back if I'm invited to sit beside you at your table and have dinner every evening."

The princess is not very keen on having a frog as her partner at table, but as the king insists on inviting him, one evening when he is sitting beside her, she throws the frog against the wall and he turns into a prince.

Joanna responded by saying:

"My inner slimy thing that lives at the bottom of the bog is not the creative side of me. In my inner voices I hear him as furious, tearing and dragging me down there. That side of me is the lost, furious, vicious child. Always active and blaming. He hates me—the part of me that wants to carry on living."

"Yes," I said, "embracing or inviting that slimy slug eating thing is not an exercise for the naïve inner person in us. It's more like the dangerous work of disposing of a bomb. But this is part of you, and if it doesn't come into dialogue, the danger is that it will get mixed up with your life, where the creature eats your food and you go down with the creature, where there is a lot of mess and chaos."

She said, "I guess I will have to start talking."

I said: "Yes, the lost child down there is willing to be told a story, and the grown-up part of you, with me beside you, will have to tell it to her. And it is a mutual experience because it includes listening to the lost child and what she has to say."

This is how we set the scene for our work.

As a Jungian psychoanalyst, I think that the process of active imagination combines the left and right sides of the brain. It opens up for new explicit and implicit emotional language and, in so doing, deepens the healing processes.

Many sessions later, Joanna told me about a dream she had had about little girls being locked up in a cellar with windows on one side. In the dream, Joanna is sitting outside and looking through the window at the furious activity of the girls making paper birds taking place inside.

When she was recounting the dream, she felt a furious manic power overwhelming her and voices blaming her for not doing enough, being clever enough, or successful enough. Our analytical work was no use, and she was just a failure. Furthermore, as her analyst, I did not really think that she was able to develop. That was her transference.

So the uneducated creature was there again.

I asked her if she could dream the dream again by imagining herself coming into contact with the girls in the damp hot cellar and talking to them.

What would she say?

She said to them, "But you have to rest, get some sleep, and eat properly with a knife and fork, and sit at a table" (like the frog).

My comment was, "So you taught them how to take care of themselves."

Yes, she said, "They had not been looked after properly when they were little."

Later we worked with her inner voices so that they could only reach her at specific hours. She told them to leave and come back the next day when walking home from work, but not to enter her apartment.

"To my surprise," she said, "they stayed outside in the open air. And one day the frog voice monster walked beside me and tried to hold my hand. Instead of shooting his imperative sentences from behind, he wanted to hold my hand and talk about how sad it was to have not been taken care of as a child."

Joanna cried, and I was moved to tears.

Analytical work can be both dangerous and difficult, and it takes courage to really feel the feelings. Words, language, images, literature, mythological fairy tales, and analytical dialogue are where things happen. In this work, it was important to articulate the words and name the frog. "The frog voice monster" became the name that we used between us, and it can be also seen from the perspective of Wittgenstein's language game concept. We created a unique dialogue in a long-standing analytical work in which the unconscious appeared in the form of voices, colours, images, affects. Giving name and form to symbols and ultimately being able to listen to the unknown within ourselves and within the frame of the elliptical dialogue is not an easy process. It means entering into the white area of the map of the elliptical dialogue. From the point of view of analytical psychology, active imagination is also rooted in the alchemical way of creating a synthesis that has the goal of creating "gold" in symbolic rather than factual understanding. The symbolic inner gold that is found and synthesised can be immensely important for the individuation process. Being open to Hermes' influence in the white area means opening up to the unknown. As Jung writes in the foreword to "The transcendent function": "How does one come to terms with the unconscious? Indirectly, it is the fundamental question, of all religions and all philosophies. For the unconscious is not this thing or that; it is the Unknown as it immediately affects us." The symbolic inner "gold" can also take the form of the unspoken.

THE IMPOSSIBLE QUESTION
OR THE MISSING BONE/LEG.

In this clinical narrative, we will meet with Helen and try to come close to what it can be like when something you have experienced in life cannot be put into words. Because no words can ever reach and touch the pain of the loss of her child, her daughter is gone forever, and this loss will forever be a part of Helen's personal history.

Helen enters with a question: "How can I survive the suicide of my daughter without being lost in guilt? Please give me an answer!"

One year ago, Karen ended her life by driving into the front of a bus. I met the whole family, but in different individual settings because their insurance gave them the right to 10 sessions each. I was open to however they wanted to meet with me. The father came first, and we continued to work together for a year. Karen's brother came for three sessions, and then finally Karen's mother, Helen, came one year after Karen's death.

"Well, Helen," I said," that is an impossible question to answer. I guess you have received a similar answer many times. It is left out, expelled. Perhaps the people you meet turn away from you with an averted face. Perhaps they do this out of fear, silent consideration, or are afraid of being regarded as clumsy, churlish, or rude. But that is of no help in your horror."

"Yes, there is silence in the outer world and a lot of voices inside myself," Helen answered.

"I can also be clumsy sometimes, in fact rather often. For example, when I was a child in a lift with my mother, a one-legged man came in, and I asked, 'What have you done to your leg? How did that happen?' It can be considered wrong and intrusive to ask such a question, but I don't think that it is wrong; in fact it can often can be liberating.'

"In fact, I often feel as if I have a torn out lost bone in my body," said Helen after a long silence.

I reflected, "And you tell also me that there are too many voices in your inner reality, as if you are carrying an invisible sack of stones on your shoulders and its name is shame and guilt. This is a human way to carry guilt and shame."

"Hmm ...," Helen responded.

"You see, I do not have a right answer for you. In the background there are too many voices and words. Perhaps you could write them down! The guilt and shame that shout and cry in the darkness. Wrestle down your despair with the help of words. But I'm sorry, Helen, that I have not answered your question. But I have answered in the only way I know now."

To our next session, Helen brought Karen's psychiatric case records. We agreed that I should keep them locked up in my office and that my task was to read them about five minutes before each session so that Helen could ask me questions about what I had read. This became our working model, and Helen continued to mourn and lament Karen, her loss, and her life. Helen wrote down the words and sentences that came to her when visiting Karen's grave, where they have conversations. The voices and words are framed in our sessions and in Helen's meeting with Karen in the graveyard. I also can see that Helen has a stronger presence in her everyday life.

The guilt and shame that were mixed up in the voices of the heavy sack enter our dialogue in the sessions. Slowly, we begin to sort out what might have been made different in the relationship with Karen and what was impossible. What kind of guilt can be seen as realistic, both from the perspective of the parents and from the perspective of the carers? The loss of a beloved child is in a category of its own and is impossible to fully comprehend. Perhaps it can only be expressed in metaphors, images and poetic language.

My experience of the dialogue with Helen in our sessions was that her self-field offered to follow her if she was brave enough to wrestle with her inner world, where the inner life of the sack could be made visible and articulated. However, some of it had to be hidden within a dark pocket of its own unknown.

If we consider Bateson's "syllogisms in metaphor" as an understanding of speaking of the unspoken for a moment we can say that:

Children are missing.

Bones are missing.

Children are bones.

This image opens up the sensory pathways and emotional gestures in our work. Bateson's preverbal analogical vision seems pertinent to the intrapsychic and interrelational elliptical dialogue. It indicates that advice and expertise are not enough and that we have to reach for connections at levels that lie beyond the scope of words. I feel that Bateson is saying that there is a hidden language that has to do with what Pascal called "reasons of the heart." Of course, when Bateson talks about syllogisms in metaphor, he does not mean that we should literally use these figures of speech, but rather that senses and feelings carry important messages about life and that the channels of thinking, reason, and logic can be untrustworthy. It is a way of trusting the senses, stay with them, listen and put them into metaphorical words from our intuition and senses. For me, his way of thinking about the unspeakable in retrospect became a perspective for a possible way of being with the impossible.

With the discovery of mirror neurons, the conclusion has been reached that there is a close and deep connection between language and action. The neuron web that is responsible for creating language is situated in the same realm as the neurons that govern action. These little cells fire off in us when we see another creature involved in an important action and when we feel touched by someone else's feelings, and vice versa (Bauer 2005). This is also why the emphasis on the wider web is so important for a psychotherapist. Not only are we required to understand the threads that link people together, we also have to become one of the threads. My first Jungian supervisor told me that if she were to remain true to the process, she had to be in touch with a sort of gyroscope inside herself. If you stay with the various kinds of modernist psychology, you will always see your job as one of building roads, putting up bridges, and getting involved in other engineering projects. That is not a bad thing in itself and can be useful, but if you move to analytical psychology, you have to be prepared to jump into the pool of the unconscious with the other creatures. This is a great equalizer and has its dangers, but at the same time it is the primary and deepest source that has the power to transform.

Let us look at the clinical vignette in which Helen poses her impossible question from the perspective of Jung's writings about The Transcendent Function (CW 8). Jung wrote this text in 1916, during his confrontation with the unconscious. This is also the year when *Septem Sermones ad Mortuos*, with its peculiar language, came into being. The Transcendent Function remained in Jung's desk for 37 years until it was found in 1953 and published in 1957 (Jung was then 82 years of age). This text is Jung's first attempt at a synthesised view of the psychic process in analytical treatment. It is also interesting because in his preface of 1958, he moves from the term unconscious to that of the unknown. The unknown as a concept creates a bridge in our understanding of how systems theory and analytical psychology can be linked. It is also very creative, because it opens up a window to philosophy, theology, and physics.

In Helen's unbearable situation, with the compelling inner voices and the stone sack of guilt and shame weighing heavily on her, there was a lot of material to come into consciousness. Giving me Karen's medical records freed Helen to allow her inner voices into the conscious realm, write them down, and begin an intrapsychic dialogue with both the voices and her inner image of Karen. The method of active imagination is helpful here, especially when practised in the safe confines of analytical work. This is how we come to terms in practice with the unconscious (CW 8 p 67). But in Jungian psychoanalytical work, active imagination is not just a manual or prescription. It is a concept that is contained by being active at the intrapsychic and interpersonal levels and is an energetic process for what lies beneath the surface of consciousness. The method is not without its dangers and should only be used under expert supervision (CW 8 p. 68). If it is practised within a holding containing frame, the psychological transcendent function will arise from the union of conscious and unconscious content. It is demanding for the relationship of the analyst and analysand, and requires an experienced assessment of the patient's ego function. There must be the possibility for the ego to integrate the meaning and the moral demands that will become visible in the deep layers of the self into the personality. The ego-self axis is of vital importance here, both for the analyst and the analysand. This is why it is so important for the analyst to continue his or her own analytical work. As an analyst, you have a deep experience of being in the borderlands and in the liminal space. This allows the psychic process to remain stable and creative.

But what is it that makes the death of a child so indescribably painful?

When Helen and I talked and let the dialogue unfold, we established a strong relationship, and she was able to move into her deep unconscious layers by listening to and writing from her inner world. Years later she could express that the loss of her child Karen is not just a loss in the wrong expectation. "We bury our parents but we do not expect to bury our children," she said, "but there is more, and maybe it is about that we give ourselves to the child. From the first gaze and touch, we have hopes and joy and fears within ourselves and for the child as well. We grow together and match our maturing, the best we can with the child's maturing. We watch the future take shape from gesture to first language of babble to dialogues. They go from dependence to more and more equality. And now she is gone. That future is destroyed. She slipped out of my arms—and was smashed. And the question keeps asking itself, 'Why did she do it?' As a mother, I stay with my helpless child while growing up. That is what mothers do. But she had great difficulties in caring for herself. And I have regrets that I shall live with. Some forgiven some not."

In the interconnectedness, in the border between Bateson's syllogisms in metaphor and Jung's transcendent function and the psychology of the transference and life and death, we can let the unheard, claiming, shouting, and whispering voices come into being.

THE DOGHOUSE REVISITED

Before concluding this chapter of clinical narratives relating to the different points of interconnectedness between analytical psychology, language theory and systems theory, we need to revisit the doghouse in Björn's world.

One day, toward the end of our work, Björn told me he had encountered the dog again. He began with this story: "I have met with the Rottweiler again, and you know what? He told me he has found a home for himself and his wife. They live in my flowerbed just outside my bedroom, and I can see them down there from my window. They have a couple of puppies."

During our analytical work, the dog was present in one form or another. It is also interesting to follow how the Rottweiler's and Björn's individuation processes ran in parallel. If we add the transference process, that was also very strong and developed from Björn's claim on me to be his all-containing mother, father, and mistress to finally end up as a housewife and mother seeing him leave home. The hermeneutical spiral movement arrived at the same point, albeit from another level of maturity. These three parallel realities existed at the same time and became visible as archetypal symbolic images.

When Jung placed himself in alchemy as a basis for his formulation of the analytical process and active imagination, he had a very systemic argument that is both interesting and relevant. It comes from his *Alchemical Studies*: "I had learned that all the greatest and most important problems of life are fundamentally insoluble. They must be so, for they express the necessary polarity inherent in every self-regulating system. They can never be solved, but only outgrown" (C. G. Jung 1968/1981 § 18) As I read, understand, and experience Jung, Bateson, and Wittgenstein, one of their meeting points is that what is experienced as a conflict, problem, or struggle is not itself the problem. The problem is the one-sided perspective and the locked-up description of the perspective. That does not mean that analysts should not be empathic to and share the pain of the patient, but rather that they should be open to the polarity within the system by keeping the balance in the elliptical dialogue. The Rottweiler inhabits abysmal fear and at the same time is able to give birth to the next generation. The frog voice monster is a power that drags the psyche down to extinction, but when it is given the words in a dialogue, it is able to establish a mutual relationship as an inner child who is always in true dialogue with a caring grown-up. Likewise, the unblocking of the unfathomable loss of a child as a forever missing bone in a mother's body by finding a metaphor for something that cannot be expressed and faced gives space for tears of mourning and lifelong grief.

PART III
THREE THEORIES IN
THE ELLIPTICAL DIALOGUE –
THE SYNTHESISING,
INTEGRATIVE PART

8. The connecting web—a kind of fishing net

Woman Holding a Balance 1664. Jan Vermeer (1632 – 1675.)
Widener Collection open access

When integrating the two theories into analytical psychology and the three theories into the map of the elliptical dialogue, this can be seen as applying a special kind of fishing net to the theoretical understanding and clinical practice. In one way or another, we always make use of our theories and transform them into analytical work. But in this intrapsychic and interpersonal dialogue within the analyst and with colleagues, it is important to formulate for oneself the deepest level of our understanding. In the case of this book, the deepest level is to ask what analytical psychology, as formulated from the beginning by C.G. Jung, sees and understands that can make points of contact possible with systems theory and language theory.

Unfortunately, psychology and its theories can be misused. Putting a psychological fishing net over a piece of art or mythological text amounts to the same thing. It is akin to covering a great piece of text with squared paper and accepting the limitations of the words that remain visible. If we cover the first verse of the Gospel of John in the same way—"In the beginning was the Word, and the... Word was with God, and the Word was God"—and accept the limitations as absolute the truth, we see a few meaningless fragments: "Int heb egin ning wast heWo rdan dthe... Word wasw with Goda ndth eWor dwas God." This kind of reading can then become a question of picking up bits and pieces here and there that dissociate and become fragments of understanding.

It is important to see that language of psychological symbols, for example in metaphors, words, images, and dialogue, also have life and that the network or web in which they are held is also a kind of metaphor in terms of the representations of human beings. To understand what it is in human existence that holds the different theoretical and clinical languages together might create a coherent wholeness of theory and praxis similar to the synthesising and differentiating movement within the ego-self axis in the elliptical dialogue. Allowing our psyches to emerge and come into being can be difficult to accept, which means that the psychological fishing net and the map of the elliptical dialogue must be used carefully if it is to plummet the depths of the human being. Only then can we create an authentic reality, where the human psyche and its meaning can be both visible to ourselves and to the world in our everyday lives. In C. G. Jung's *The Red Book* (p. 229) in the first part called Liber Primus, this transcendent perspective is clarified and understood as a fundamental condition for analytical psychology.

"But I did not consider that the spirit of the depths from time immemorial and for all the future possesses a greater power than the spirit of this time, who changes with the generations. The spirit of the depths has subjugated all pride and arrogance to the power of judgment. He took away my belief in science, he robbed me of the joy of explaining and ordering things, and he let devotion to the ideals of this time die out in me. He forced me down to the last and simplest things." (C.G. Jung 2009 p. 229)

C.G. Jung wrote this over 100 years ago, in 1915. In his own life he had to plummet the depths in order to wake up. *The Red Book* illustrates this process in images and relationships. The language that is most suitable for this is metaphors and poetry. The Swedish poet Tomas Tranströmer (1931-2015) who won the Nobel Prize in Literature in 2011, gives a sense of the transcendent movement in the first verse of his poem *Prelude*.

"Waking up is a parachute jump from dreams." (Tranströmer in New Collected Poems 1997/2011.)

Literature, poetry, and art are bound up with psychology. Psychology and the arts can facilitate changes in how we see ourselves, our lives, and the world. In the green elliptical line, this intermediate liminal landscape, it can be fruitful to see psychology as a clearing, an opening space that reveals a space, rather than a field that produces knowledge. In Jung's *The Red Book* (2009), this can be explored and discovered in regarding every word as a door with a possible key to it. Artwork such as texts, poetry, and paintings have keys that we can find in our own inner and outer realities. Likewise, in the different psychological fields of understanding of the human psyche and also in systems theory, language philosophy, and analytical psychology, everyone has an individual key that can be tried in different doors to see which one it fits. Meeting another person in a relational dialogue is very similar. Finding the key that opens the door, reveals new perspectives, and connects the ego-self planes is important and imperative.

The following illustration connects the three theories and their main contributions to the elliptical dialogue. It can be seen as a kind of fishing net that facilitates a dialogue with our personal and professional individuation.

Points of Contact in the Connecting Web - Figure Created by Gunilla Midbøe

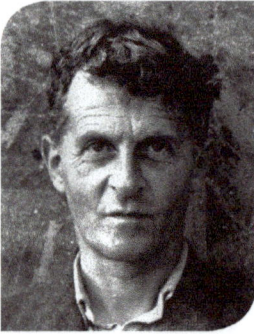

Wittgenstein's Contribution

- The limits of my language mean the limits of my world.
- What we cannot speak about we must pass over in silence.
- Duck-rabbit

Bateson's Contribution

- We live in a world that is only made of relationships. The hand metaphor.
- Metaphor is the language of relationships.
- Pattern that connects is metapattern.
- A difference that makes a difference over time is change.

Jung's Contribution

- Inner and outer reality equally real.
- The transcedent function as a synthesising perspective.
- The dyadic nature of the deep affective exploration of the self.
- Principium individuationis.

PART III
THREE THEORIES IN
THE ELLIPTICAL DIALOGUE –
THE SYNTHESISING,
INTEGRATIVE PART

9. Systems theory—Bateson's contribution and its effect on dialogue in today's analytical psychology

The essential idea in systems theory is that all things are connected. For Bateson, the view of the living world as a unity requires a change in the understanding of our sense of self. The self is immanent, both in the body and in all the informational systems that link us to the wider environment. From this perspective, Jung's concept of the self joins Bateson's view of the self to enrich each other. As mentioned earlier, it was Bateson's reading of Jung's *Septem Sermones ad Mortuos* that formed a bridge and bow between mind and nature. It seems that Bateson's use of the idea of an ecological "god" may have been inspired by the discovery of this text, which was given to him by the Jungian analyst Jane Wheelwright. In his review (Brand 1974), Bateson describes "this tiny book" as "the greatest achievement of Jung's life—the turning point in a long battle ... the moment for a new (or return to a very old) natural history of Man-God-Cosmos." Jung's presentation of the Seven Sermons to the Dead as a work of the ancient gnostic thinker Basilides may have struck a chord with Bateson. Basilides proposes Abraxas as the creator of construction and destruction. The nature of Abraxas is ambivalent, with the poles of life and death both present. Bateson may have found a metaphorical reference of divinity here that he needed as a link for his understanding of the earth's ecological systems.

It is also worth noting that the understanding of the collective unconscious in analytical psychology has important similarities to Bateson's idea about an all-embracing mental system.

As early as 1970, Bateson lectured on his idea of divinity:

"The cybernetic epistemology which I have offered you would suggest a new approach. The individual mind is immanent also in pathways and messages outside the body; and there is a larger Mind of which the individual mind is only a sub-system. This larger Mind is comparable to God and is perhaps what some people mean by 'God,' but it is still immanent in the total interconnected social system and planetary ecology. ... What I am saying expands mind outwards ... a certain humility becomes appropriate, tempered by the dignity or joy of being a part of something much bigger. A part—if you will—of God" (Charlton 2008, p. 164).

Just as in analytical psychology, Bateson transcended all kinds of dualism: between mind and body, mind and matter, humans and nature, and eventually between divinity and the world. As systems theory sees it, our consciousness is just a small arc in the wider currents and loops of the knowing that interconnects us. The larger circuits in which we participate are the "pattern which connects." The values that emerge from this understanding of the self and its wider connecting web are ethical and normative in nature. You could say that certain moral values are required for the existence of systemic harmony and unity. Here, we enter into the therapeutic considerations of the elliptical dialogue. The respect for integrity is an important part of the dialogue. Keeping the dialogue in the therapeutic context means being aware of the creative liminal space for relationship and words. This also involves an ethical standpoint. We all participate in the lives of other beings, which makes us indebted to them and responsible for them. Ignoring that connection would be akin to damaging ourselves, in that we would exclude the participation we need. The needs of others emerge as being covalent and equivalent with our own. This means that our sense of self will be widened to include all our interactions with others. Cybernetic stability requires this broader base, as well as the understanding that we live in a unified world. Survival on the planet requires a shift to this view. This is the ethical standpoint of Bateson's systems theory, which is not apparent when reading about systems theory. Sometimes, from a systems perspective, there can be a feeling of coldness and alienation from ethical values. This is also relevant for the values of the feminine and the masculine, and is a criticism of systems theory. However, here I want to point out that, for Bateson, ethics and preserving connections within the system were important.

Theoretical development is continuous and today we have the concepts of first-, second-, and third-order cybernetics. Recently in analytical psychology, complex adaptive systems (CAS) have been used to understand Jung's thoughts about synchronistic energies (Cambray and Carter 2004. Cambray 2009).

From the perspective of family and individual therapy, first- and second-order cybernetics are related to the observer's position in relationship to the system. In first-order cybernetics, the therapist, or observer, is seen as someone outside the system producing ideas of change and suggesting interventions in order to bring about change. In cognitive behaviour therapy, this position is used deliberately as a way of helping the patient eliminate undesirable behaviour, thoughts or attitudes. Cognitive programs are created for the patient to follow. The therapist is more like a coach or counselor for better everyday life quality. The second-order cybernetic sees the observer as part of the therapeutic/analytic system of treatment. Participation in the system is deliberately interactive with all the members in the setting. The therapist/ analyst role changes, as do the members of the system, the interactions, and the relationships. As in Bateson's metaphor, you do not only have four fingers and a thumb on your hand, but have first and foremost the interconnecting patterns of four relationships.

When Björn showed me his Father Murder collage, these relationships between us were strongly challenged. What followed was a rupture that changed us both, not only our analytical work but also our respective lives. I became more conscious of my enormous power as an analyst and the ability to both heal and cause damage. In this experience, the system, our holding relationship, based on trust was strongly challenged and had to allow for the affects of rage, fear, shame, joy, despair, guilt, eagerness, grudge, jealousy, and affection. Ultimately, there was room for resilience and forgiveness. All these affects had to be expressed and explored as they emerged in our interactive field. In this struggle, holding the inner map of the elliptical dialogue helped, although I did not (and no one can) teleologically know whether our system would be resilient and have reciprocity enough to cope with this sudden and surprising enactment. In this work, both attachment theory and affect theory are applicable. With Björn's history of negative attachment, it was understandable that he was in a regressed ego-self state when entering with the image. It is interesting to note that the image contains a mythical representation of the archer releasing his arrow to the highest point in his complex—the father. Björn was very proud of his work! When working through the ruptures in the blue frame and the green elliptical line, it was important to express all the affects. In the moment of enactment, my own arrow was also fired from the strengthened bow. It was as though the arrow from my bow, like a countertransference reaction of pulling back, hit Björn right in the wound of his mother complex. All the affects that he expressed were akin to a profuse bleeding. It took many hours and many meetings for us to work through this experience and at a meta-level, where it was possible to put his perspective and later my perspective into words. This was probably due to the containing experience of the resilience in our relationship and, metaphorically, in the mutual resilience of our respective bows and arrows. Understanding and consciousness need time and space for the self to emerge, especially when, as in every system, there are irrational Hermes tricksters running around.

GENERAL SYSTEMS THEORY (GST), CYBERNETICS, COMPLEX ADAPTIVE SYSTEMS (CAS) AND ANALYTICAL PSYCHOLOGY.

General Systems Theory (GST) is the interdisciplinary study of systems in general that can help to form principles for the system. The term originates from Ludwig von Bertalanffy's (1968) *General System Theory: Foundations, Development, Applications*. A central topic of systems theory is self-regulating systems, which in the strict sense means that the system is self-correcting through feedback. These systems are found in nature, including the physiological system of our bodies, in local and global ecosystems, in the climate, and in human learning processes.

Cybernetics has been defined in a variety of ways by a number of people from various disciplines. The threads of cybernetics were woven in the late 1800s and led to Norbert Wiener's work titled *Cybernetics* (1948) and later von Bertalanaffy's *General Systems Theory* (1968). It can be said that cybernetics arose from the field of engineering and general systems theory (GST) from biology, with the two fields mutually influencing each other.

It is important to realize that cybernetics drawn into psychology also has the history of a wide range of definitions in its background. For example, attachment theory is drawn from cybernetics into psychology and concerned with how human beings form long-term relationships. Also, from attachment theory, Tomkins' affect theory comes naturally as a theory concerned with instincts. Affect theory is based on biology and deals with the human ability to express fundamental affects in the face, body, and behaviour when the individual and the relational systems are in contact with another human being in the environment.

In both first- and second-order cybernetics, we find Bateson's contribution to psychology and the connection with the larger earth system as a connection of man to nature. In this system, the ability of living organisms to interconnect in relationships and experience a spiritual dimension of life are important factors. Bateson was a biologist and therefore fascinated with nature's order in things. For example, he studied the communicational language of dolphins and also the conch, with its spiral shell configuration. For him, the latter was an example of patterns connecting and giving life to wider patterns. If you put the conch close to your ear, it is possible to imagine the sound of the sea.

First-order cybernetics is about observed systems, whereas second-order cybernetics is about observing systems. When talking about a third-order cybernetics, it means that it embraces both first- and second-order cybernetics. Third-order cybernetics can be seen as a meta-level, with a greater emphasis on language as a co-construction of reality and communication. In systemic literature, it is often formulated as "the problem is not the problem, the problem is the description of the problem." This is to indicate that the emphasis should be put on language and metaphors as a way of opening up new perspectives of reality, which can be experienced within the observing system and as a view of the interrelated reality of it. From the perspective of analytical psychology, language should be understood in a wider sense and not be reduced to specific words. On looking more closely at it, language forms and contributes to the map and territory of Jungian psychoanalysis.

Cybernetics, catastrophe theory, chaos theory, and complexity theory all have the common goal of explaining complex systems consisting of a large number of mutually interacting and interrelated parts. As all these "C" theories emphasize different tools and methodologies, it is difficult to imagine studying such complex systems without using a computer.

Skype settings and the Internet can potentially be used to create an analytical room, and modern technology increasingly offers new possibilities for analysis. For example, Skype allows the analyst and the analysand to communicate by voice and video. "Co-tuning" to work in Skype can be a ritual that even deepens the analytical relationship. This process depends on the way the dialogue is perceived and understood, and the personalities of the analyst and analysand. The interactive field, the entire Hermes area, is also available in the outer reality, perhaps even in a seductive way. In my own experience, both as an analysand and analyst, it is important to first meet face-to-face before using a video camera. Meeting in the temenos (the sacred precinct) of the consulting room first and having the experience of the holding frame of the room is also important before moving onto Skype sessions. It is within this setting that the analytical alliance is created.

But I also think that we can make new nests for temenos when we extend our analytical space to Skype. It can complement physical meetings but should then be mutually explored and defined by both the analyst and the analysand. A frank exchange of how the experience is felt in the body, mind, and relationship is important too. The body then becomes an indicator of the analyst's and analysand's co-tuning in the analytic process. Handled with care, I think that Skype can deepen the analytical experience and give analysands access to analytical treatment in an extended way. If the analysand for some reason is unable to travel, Skype can be used to maintain the analytical process so that it is not interrupted. In training situations, Skype is used in training analyses with candidates and in supervision, although the hours required for meeting in real life and for meeting on Skype are strictly regulated. The development of analytical psychology in different parts of the world would not have been very successful if the Internet had not facilitated training analyses, supervision, and webinar lectures. But again, it is essentially dependent on the ethical responsibility of the analyst to be careful and moderate the sessions. Used in this way, Skype can facilitate an awareness of subtle energies and unconscious layers of the psyche that can make it possible to try new paths and enhance the relationship between the analyst and analysand. For example, one of my clients, Joanna, (see Part II, chapter *The Frog Voice Monster*) when working with the voices of the frog voice monster, found it helpful to read her dialogue in the Skype session and distinguish between the imperative, punishing voices and her own ego, her own "I." She said she would not have had the courage to do so in an early live session. With Skype, she did not feel quite so exposed when reading. Later in our work with active imagination, the *frog voice monster* developed into a more mature creature, with the ability to mourn and feel sadness about how as a child Joanna had been treated and neglected by her mother and how these experiences had led to an inner world of devaluation. When this deep, painful dialogue was written down, she was able to read it after a few Skype sessions. I listened and encouraged mutual reflections on the dialogue, which led to her crying about and mourning her childhood. My first thought was that Skype would be too close, with our faces exposed on video, but she experienced the screen as a protective area, and we agreed that when she was reading the dialogues, she would turn around, look down and not show her face to me. I could see her back and listen carefully to her reading. In my reflection I thought that she used the screen similar to the couch. For her, this felt like protection, while I was able to listen and allow her this shelter. This could not have been done in such a distinct way if we had meet physically in my practice. This is an example of the white Hermes space being able to moderate with the aid of new technology and the Internet.

Complex adaptive systems (CAS) are special complex systems. They are complex in that they are diverse and composed of multiple, interconnected elements and are adaptive in that they can change and learn from experience. The term complex adaptive system was coined at the interdisciplinary Santa Fe Institute (SFI) by John H. Holland, Murray Gell-Mann, and others. An alternative conception of complex adaptive (and learning) systems, methodologically at the interface between natural and social science, has been presented by Kristo Ivanov in terms of hypersystems.

In the context of analytical psychology, complex adaptive systems have been explored in the essay *Synchronicity as Emergence* by Joseph Cambray (Cambray, Carter 2004) and in the book by Cambray titled *Synchronicity—Nature and Psyche in an Interconnected Universe* (2009.) From the perspective of Jungian psychoanalysis, this phenomenon is described as the experience of transcendence. It is also described as moments of intense emotion and affect, and thus as synchronistic events. Also in analytical psychology, Murray Stein explores these intense events (Stein 2014, 2015) and frames them in the context of contemporary spirituality and the expressions of mutual self-fields that connect in synchronistic events. In the chapter *Not Just a Butterfly* (Stein 2014), we can follow the butterfly and its appearance in a set of meaningful events in a strong relationship, transforming from life to a reality beyond death. The butterfly metaphor is not just a metaphor, but the transcendent reality of inner and outer experience in the synchronistic events of a lived reality. Here, I think, analytical psychology adds the important concept of the individual and the shared relational experience of psyche to general systems theory (GST) and to complex adaptive systems (CAS.) The personal openness to these synchronistic events is both healing and meaningful, and promotes further individuation. What Stein seems to be advocating in his book is the possibility of development toward a contemporary spirituality by *Minding the Self* (2014.) We can all be open to synchronistic events by consciously paying attention to our inner and outer realities and seeing them as equally real. This awareness and the vigilant mindfulness of the transcendent ability of one's ego-self axis bring meaningfulness and deep individuation into personal and collective life.

I'm not sure whether this is the case for CAS. These systems change without individual relationships, and the change appears within clusters that merge and move toward the edge of chaos. When breaking through the limit, they go into another complex system. This change just happens. As Cambray writes in the end of the essay:

> "To conclude, many features of synchronistic experience can be reconsidered in the light of contemporary science as a form of psychological emergence. Heralding the constellation of supraordinate self-organizing states, synchronicities offer valuable clues to the unfolding of the psyche, or individuation but must be treated as value-neutral, i.e., in themselves they do not convey direction to consciousness. Instead, this can only come from reflective, ethical struggles with meaning which we subjectively attribute to these occurrences." (In Cambray and Carter 2004 p.244)

This important statement brings us back to the intermediate section between science and psychology, and also to the beginning of this chapter; we have to look for keys that can open doors of words into our individuation processes. Personally, I need the keys of relationship, words, and nonverbal language to receive and see something more than the expected and the familiar. There is more to explore with our five senses, and even more in a relationship that has the potential to grow in consciousness. Imagine what five senses can discover, then imagine what two people with five senses can explore in the elliptical dialogue relationship.

Again, the white area of Hermes can be seen as a connecting principle of how systems work. This might seem like a free-floating energy that is both destructive and constructive depending on how it is judged by the participant observer within the system. We can blame the other through our own projections, and of course the other affects how I act and how my conditions develop. But being able to see and integrate my shadow figures, the consciousness can develop and become a potential for development, even in the most difficult of circumstances.

In terms of how the human brain functions, the discovery of the GPS gene in mice by Nobel Laureates Edward I. and May-Britt Moser was an important breakthrough. The ability and need for the brain to order and map are essential for humans. However, our ability to differentiate between the given and agreed context of what is optimal for the situation is also necessary. Hermes has to be both known and related to. No wonder that the early alchemists relied on Hermes to produce gold in the era when science, psychology, and spirituality had not yet been discerned as separate disciplines.

When trying to incorporate the life of language into the elliptical dialogue, certain boundaries need to be recognised. It is often suggested that if we can describe a defined reality "out there," it can be better communicated and understood. In terms of imagery, the arrow of psychic energy will be pointed toward the outer reality. This is an important way of understanding the power of language. When Björn was able to tell a coherent story about the father complex, he could fire the arrow toward the destructive father, as shown in the illustration Father Murder in Part II. But a reverse-arrow energy force is also at work here, which points toward a new inner reality that is formed within and with the reacting body. In Björn's case, this reverse-arrow energy pointed toward the integration of the other polarity of the father archetype. It became possible to integrate the spiritual father energy within and still keep the consequences of the devastating father in mind. This new inner reality then formed a stable ground for holding the immense tensions of the extreme polarities of the father archetype. In effect, Björn was the archer who could fire the arrow from his bow toward a new wholeness of his individuation journey. My experience is that by talking, listening, reflecting, acting, dreaming, and imagining, dialogical language can create a narrative that is capable of changing our inner and outer realities.

PART III
THREE THEORIES IN
THE ELLIPTICAL DIALOGUE –
THE SYNTHESISING,
INTEGRATIVE PART

10. Language Theory— Wittgenstein's contribution and how dialogue is used in analytical psychology.

In psychotherapy, we constantly find ourselves in a relationship with the other, for example in the inner and outer reality and the intersection of minds. An awareness of these subprocesses of mind is important when formulating a theory, a hypothesis, or an understanding of what is going on in the consulting room. In this part of the book, the focus is on language and dialogue. The word "focus" has different meanings. In geometry, the focus is a fixed point from which an ellipse, parabola, or other curve is drawn (Oxford English Dictionary 2012). The noun "focuser" has its origins in Latin and means "domestic hearth." The focus of a house or household was originally the name for the central hearth. In Greek mythology, the goddess of the hearth is Hestia. This is the place where the fire was never allowed to die down or go out. The hearth, as the focus of dialogue, language, the exchange of all kinds of communication, is a place of warmth. It is also a good metaphor for language and the exchange of dynamic interconnections and mental processes, in terms of the forming of words, speech, listening, and reflective activity. The green elliptical line is also a focus, although here the focus shifts from separate boundaries to an integrated dynamic process. What flows between and along the line and how this is made conscious and accessible is facilitated by the dialogic language used and by the sense of togetherness created in the analytical setting.

The Oxford Dictionary (2012) defines language as "the means of human communication, consisting of the use of spoken or written words in a structured way." This is an overarching definition of language. In this chapter, it is important to distinguish between the different levels of language. At one level, language is used in the context of a defined discipline. We are schooled in different disciplines and their associated language games (Wittgenstein 1953). Authorities—the masters of the disciplinary discourses—are central to every discipline, in this particular context the *language games* of C.G. Jung, Gregory Bateson and Ludwig Wittgenstein. But this is not enough to be aware of the particular language games, because we are engaged in a practical analytical context as well. This is a fruitful and living relationship that combines scientific language and the analytical language game. The latter is not a game that can be learned exclusively by studying the master's different voices. It has to be experienced face-to-face in the consulting room. However, the language game of academics is not excluded. On the contrary, there is pressure to incorporate this language in the analytical meeting. This has to be done in a way that engages other levels of the self. It is the connection of the scientific and analytical levels that I visualize in the elliptical dialogue. The analytical level engages our bodies and our ways of acting in the sense that perceptual rather than cognitive changes are crucial. Wittgenstein's emphasis on language games and gestures that precede words and language, and Bakhtin's (1997) construction of what he calls the dialogical imagination are important contributions.

In *The Poetics of Reverie* (1960/1969), the French philosopher Gaston Bachelard (1884-1963) provides extraordinary meditations on the relation between consciousness and the world. He demonstrates the potential of awareness, thus distinguishing relaxation from the kind of reverie that "poetry puts on the right track, the track of expanding consciousness." He is also influenced by C.G. Jung in the basic assumptions of this last significant work:

"Of all the schools of contemporary psychoanalysis, that of C.G. Jung has shown most clearly that the human psyche is, in its primitive state, androgynous. For Jung, the subconscious self is not a repressed consciousness, it is not made of forgotten memories; it is primary nature. Whoever speaks of androgyneity is brushing the depths of his own sub-consciousness with a double antenna. One thinks he is telling a story, but the story is interesting to such an extent that it becomes psychology happening" (Bachelard, 1960/1969, p. 59).

I can clearly hear Bachelard's words echoing in Gregory Bateson's review when reading Jung's *Septem Sermones ad Mortuos*:

"This book is difficult to read. It is (of course) a sort of poetry and therefore almost impossible to be reviewed and analysed in prose. And Jung's views clearly changed as he wrote, even in the three or four days of the writing he was in a state of transition.

The book is a progress from macrocosm to microcosm and is a description of the landscape at various stages of that progress" (Part I).

Also, when using language from our bodily experience, the French feminist, philosopher, and writer Hélène Cixous is important. In her most influential essay, *Le rire de la Meduse* (1975), she encourages women all over the world to engage in their own bodies and document them in a new *écriture feminine*.

For both Bachelard and Cixous, poetic language and feminine language are clearly androgynous. Bachelard sees the two psychological instances, animus and anima, as essential for reverie. He also says that it is by coordinating reveries on reverie that he hopes to constitute a "Poetics of reverie." For him, a poetics of reverie is a poetics of the anima. The deepest and most profound layer of language he places beneath and beyond the dualism of anima and animus within every human being. "When the reverie is truly profound, the being who comes to dream within us is our *anima*" (Bachelard 1960/1969, p. 62).

Cixous expresses herself in a similar way when constructing the other bisexuality. She creates and finds her own erotic universe. To her, bisexuality means each individual's exploration of the presence of both genders in oneself, i.e., a nonexclusion of difference or either of the genders. I understand it as the development and coexistence of both animus and anima in every person, regardless of being a man or a woman. This acceptance of both forms the starting point and place for the writing and language processes in our feminine and masculine bodies.

Boundless unspoken language also engaged Wittgenstein. Both in his early work *Tractatus Logico-Philosophicus* and in his later work *Philosophical Investigations*, it was clear to him that everything we see and can mentally grasp cannot be put into words. "Whereof one cannot speak, thereof one must be silent" and "What we cannot speak about we must pass over in silence" are famous phrases in *Tractatus Logico-Philosophicus*.

It is Wittgenstein's passion for seeing, not thinking, that corresponds to Jung's famous words in his case study of individuation with Miss X, that the eye is the key to the process.

However, according to Monk (1990), Wittgenstein made it clear in private conversations and correspondence that he believed that the things about which we have to be silent were the most important. For Wittgenstein, thinking and understanding were paramount. Like Jung, Wittgenstein firmly believed that our dreams present us with a series of images.

Wittgenstein was inspired by the Polish-born American psychologist Joseph Jastrow (1863-1944) and his book Fact and Fable in Psychology (1900). Jastrow was interested in optical illusions, and in his book he included an image of a duck-rabbit head. Wittgenstein used this image to illustrate the use of the word "to see" in *Philosophical Investigations* (p. 223).

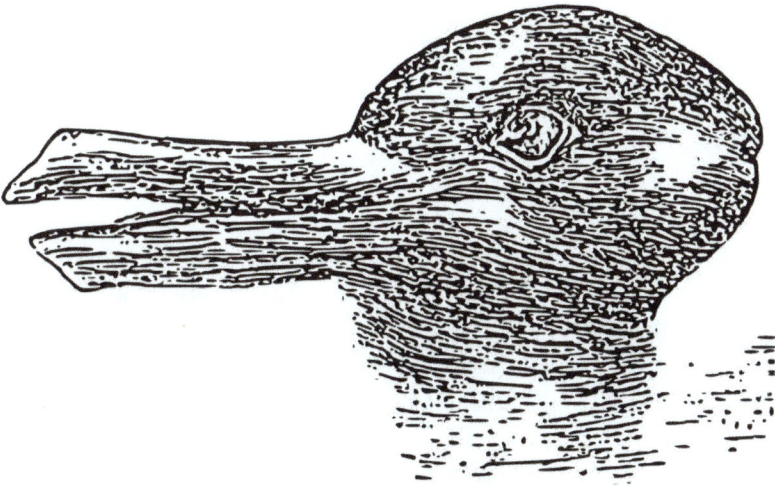

Duck-Rabbit Head - Openclipart public domain. Source: Jastrow, J. (1899). The mind's eye. Popular Science Monthly, 54, 299-312

The discussion about the use of the word "to see" and its correspondence to Jung's central thinking, in this case Miss X and the eye forming the key to the analytical process, is very relevant to analytical work. In both Wittgenstein's and Jung's thinking, double aspects of seeing are important. When we as analysts see something in an inner dialogical imagination, in an outer-presented dream image, and in an analysand's narrative, we need to pay attention to it. The word "see" can be used in different ways in the duck-rabbit example. One is: "What do you see here?"—"I see this (and then give a description or reproduce the drawing); and the other: "I see a similarity between these two figures." If my dialogical partner can also clearly see the similarity, and perhaps something more, our dialogue can develop from this dual seeing. How we give expression to the alternation, variation, and fluctuation of the aspect paves the way for a *new* perception and consciousness. Wittgenstein calls this experience "to give attention to the aspect." One of his conclusions is that it is important to differentiate between "continuously seeing" an aspect and to see an aspect suddenly "being revealed." I can see a rabbit, I can see a duck. I can say, "I see a similarity between those two faces." I can also say that I see *this* and then give a description of the duck or the rabbit. When the aspect alternation is at hand, the whole situation changes. When an aspect in Wittgenstein's sense hits us, it seems to be a mixed experience of seeing and thinking. This exchange gives birth to a surprise, an astonishment and the people in the elliptical dialogue being amazed. This experience is very different from that of recognition.

Let us now apply the above discussion to the elliptical dialogue of Björn and myself, and the different images and narratives of the father that he brought to our sessions.

THE FATHER REVISITED

Reading about Björn's image of his father is provocative. We could say: "Well this is his image and story of the father, and no one can be all that evil and punish his children in this way, not just so … surely there is another image and narrative as well?" In our analytical work, we often meet these kinds of one-sided images at the beginning. It is a challenge to keep and hold this in a dialogical narrative within the elliptical dialogue. A careful moderation has to be made to balance between *telling and narrating* and *listening and reflecting*. In theory, it is the difference between a dialogical and monological narrative, although in the consulting room this is a crisscross experience. When Björn arrived for a session with drawings of his father with a square face, dressed in a neat suit, and holding a whip with a Nazi swastika attached, it was the monological Björn who talked and reacted. To me, he seemed to be locked into himself and closed to my responses. Being dialogical in this situation meant listening to and reflecting on an inner dialogical and "withness" (being both a witness and being with) position. The challenge here was to avoid falling into the same position as Björn, namely getting into a monological and aboutness thinking and reflecting that preserved the image of the father and so that it could not be touched. At the same time, it was important to pay attention to Björn's way of seeing. However, to me, seeing Björn's father drawing and listening to his narrative made me think about the duck-rabbit image and how an expression of an aspect can rise within me, Björn, and our dialogue.

During Björn's narrative, I was struck by his words and indeed tuned myself into them as one does when reading poetry. He could say things like: "The Rottweiler tells me to stand still—how can one live with such tensions inside?" "My father said to us: 'Yes I'm brutal with you but that is because I love you so much.'" He could say: "On this earth, we live our lives between executioners and angels—this makes me scream inside, and I'm full of pain." He could also refer to literature and art, especially the major Norwegian playwright, theatre director, and poet, Henrik Ibsen (1828-1906) and his play *The Wild Duck* (1884). Björn identified his own family as living a lie, like the family in the play. One of the famous quotes from the play comes from Dr. Relling, who has built up and maintained the lies on which the family is founded: "Deprive the average human being of his life-lie, and you rob him of his happiness.'" Concerning art, Björn constantly referred to the French symbolist painter Odilon Redon (1840-1916) and especially his lithograph albums, *The Temptation of Saint Anthony* (1888, 1896).

I was struck by Björn's use of certain words to describe his father, such as "ridåhalaren" (the curtain puller), when everything turned black. He also said: "The difference between good and evil is the smile in the gaze. When this smile dies, then man becomes evil.' This was the face of my father."

One day he came with a written text beginning "The Rottweiler dream continues—in spite of the uncomfortable position they keep standing like this week after week. When six months had elapsed, Björn came to the conclusion that the dog was right:

"You are right, we should stay here and stand still.

"The dog heaved a deep sigh and slid down to the ground. He shook himself and then ran to his water bowl. He drank and drank, looking up now and again at Björn with a sour gaze.

"But anyway, we can have excursions, can't we?" Björn wondered. "Then the Rottweiler did something he had not done for six months—it wagged its tail."

This image became the bridge that both transformed and discharged Björn's aggression in his work with the father complex—a transformation that developed into the extended title of the image of *Father Murder to Father Murder/ A Fairy Tale just a Fairy Tale*. In this transformation the image of the father was also transformed by paying attention to the alternation aspect (holding the duck-rabbit image in fluctuation) after first focusing on the description of the father and following the narrative of a changing father image at a personal, archetypal, and spiritual level. The new title mirrors this bi-focal seeing aspect in language. In analytical work, words can have a poetic function. In Björn's context, the word "father" developed as a set of signposts staking out a journey over a shared landscape of possible places to go. In this sense, the words do something more than "picture" or represent the landscape. The words point toward possible shared realities "beyond." Wittgenstein's idea that "understanding a sentence is much more akin to understanding a theme in music than one may think" (1953, no. 527) helps me to slow down and keep the moment alive in and between sessions. Analytical work and a psychodynamic approach to psychotherapy are unique in that they create a frame for the slowing down of life's experiences and where careful attention can be paid to the intonation of words and sentences.

With the "father" in mind, it was important in the sessions with Björn to look at the different narratives, words, and sentences poetically, empathise and to try to introduce dialogical words when his monological discourse became repetitive. "How can a father be present in our lives?" Slowly, he began to tell me about his paternal grandfather. In Norwegian, the word for grandfather is "bestefar" (best father), which he was for Björn. From this psychogenetic work, we could follow the signposts of father toward the spiritual father. Björn struggled a lot with the Fifth Commandment: Honour thy father and thy mother. Gradually, the representational meaning of the word father became visible. One important signpost was when Björn dreamt that he was about to be buried in the same grave as his mother and father. He found this impossible and then heard a voice telling him that he could be buried in the same grave as his grandfather and grandmother if he wished. The voice continued: "Honouring your father and mother can be done in many ways, and we are all children of fathers and mothers." This dream came at a time in the analysis when the spiritual dimension of the father archetype was at the fore and Björn was concerned about finding a new home for his religious and spiritual expression. In this search, he made contact with a congregation that Björn experienced as being tolerant of diversity.

In connection with this movement of the father image from the personal to the archetypal level and the integration of language theory in analytical psychology in the map of the elliptical dialogue, it is important to revisit the ego-self axis in the map from a new angle, i.e., from the perspective of empathy. In *Paperback Oxford English Dictionary* (1979/2012), "empathy" is defined as the ability to understand and share the feelings of other people. Without empathy, we could not be able to work in analytical practice. But how does or should an analyst demonstrate empathy? In Erich Neumann's earlier-mentioned essay, *The psyche and the reality planes* (Neumann 1952/1989), he attempts to construct a changed model for humanity, and especially our psychic personality, in the world. When considering his diagram or model from the perspective of empathy, we can reflect on what is appropriate empathy in the elliptical dialogue with an analysand. The two different ego-self axes work from different positions and at the same time are connected in their self planes and ego positions. Empathy in relationship to the self planes prepares the ground for developing and promoting individuation in both the analyst and the analysand. There may be a temptation to put too much empathy at the ego level of dialogue. If this is done without balance and grounding in the self planes, we will only skim the surface. True empathy must have its roots in the self planes and be directed toward the analysand's development of the self. This directed empathy includes tolerance on the part of the analyst for a deepening of the individuation process. A truly ethical attitude needs to be rooted in analytical psychology that includes timing and introducing a dialogical discourse that is directed toward the self planes of each individual. Too much ego empathy tends to reinforce the ego's tendency toward projective processes and can lead to difficulties in working with assimilating shadow behaviour.

My pulling back from Björn and his attempted embrace when entering the practice room with the *Father Murder* image needed to be reflected on — as always after the event. It was only when the resulting rage, disappointment, shame, and guilt had subsided that we could begin to explore Björn's aggression and eagerness to take what he wanted and I could challenge his demands for me to reveal personal details. It was as though he had to demonstrate childish and equal rights behaviour in order to grow into a true dialogue and see that these were not the most important issues. The main issue was actually to promote the individuation process. But work like this is necessary with ruptures, because ruptures are often a natural part of close relationships. The main thing is that they can be made conscious in the dialogue and in each of the participants. It was after this mutual experience and working at many different and complex levels that the *Father Murder* image emerged also as *A Fairy Tale Just A Fairy Tale*. Björn commented: "This image contains in one sense our whole analytical work, and there is an ongoing dialogue between the two titles. "But for now this image, with all its narratives contained within, is my ongoing life story, for the moment named as a *Fairy Tale* but with lightness and darkness within."

For me, continuous supervision means creating an ethical space in which I am able to examine my own shadow sides. This was also necessary in my work with Björn. In parallel, my supervisor's empathy with my own self plane and individuation process was crucial for my development as an analyst and for my personage as a whole. What we call transference and parallel processes are important here, and in the next chapter of this section, I would like to explore how the transference relationship was expressed in the analytical work with Björn and how analytical psychology is integrated in the map of the elliptical dialogue.

PART III
THREE THEORIES IN
THE ELLIPTICAL DIALOGUE –
THE SYNTHESISING,
INTEGRATIVE PART

11. Analytical Psychology—Jung's contributions to the elliptical dialogue.

One of Jung's major contributions to depth psychology is that he sees the unconscious as fundamental to the human psyche. With this in mind, he attributes the unconscious with certain qualities. In CW 6 *Psychological Types* § 837- 843, under definitions 56. Jung explained "unconscious" this way:

> "The concept of the *unconscious* is for me an exclusively *psychological* concept...In my view the unconscious is a psychological borderline concept, which covers all psychic contents or processes that are not conscious, i.e., not related to the ego (q.v.) in any perceptible way. My justification for speaking of the existence of unconscious processes at all is derived simply and solely from experience... We can distinguish a personal unconscious, comprising all the acquisitions of personal life...the mythological

associations, the motifs and images that can spring up anew anytime anywhere, independently of historical tradition or migration. I call these contents the *collective unconscious…* unconscious psychic activity produces dreams, fantasies (q.v.)…A dream presents itself to us; we do not consciously create it. Conscious reproduction, or even the perception of it, certainly alters the dream in many ways, without, however, doing away with the basic fact of the unconscious source of creative activity."

In the map of the elliptical dialogue, the notion that the unconscious contains the self planes is crucial. This also reflects my own experience of analytical work, as an analysand, an analyst, a supervisee, and a supervisor. In this section, I would like to explore the relationship between the analysand and the analyst and that between the supervisor and supervisee from the perspective of what is generally called transference and countertransference. Dividing the analytical relationship in this way makes it more theoretically adaptable. The three images below (*The Little Goddesses with Birds' Heads, Facing the Void and The Flying Carpet*) and one crucial dream (The Conference Dream) will illustrate the analytical relationship with Björn at the transference level.

The Little Goddesses with Birds' Heads -
Photo reprinted with permission from Björn

The Little Goddesses with Birds' Heads was one of the first transference images that Björn brought to our analytical sessions. We had taken a summer break, and the first year of our analytical work was over. During that year, the father complex had been very present but had not been fully discharged and sufficiently worked through. The rupture in the session when he entered with the Father Murder image had not yet taken place, which meant that I was worshipped and regarded as a goddess. The message on the back of the image read: "These goddesses with birds' heads kept me occupied while you were away. They can also be found in a cave painting in the Sahara Desert that is estimated to be about 5,000 years old." I thanked him for the beautiful image, and when I asked him what he thought about it, he said; "Well, birds and gods cross borders in time and space, and they simply made me endure our break." I said I was happy to see him again. He then started to tell me about the pain he felt during our three-week separation and how this had reminded him of being shut up in the wardrobe with the moon shining through the small window. The work with the father and mother complexes continued.

In the *Tavistock Lectures—On the Theory and Practice of Analytical Psychology*, which Jung delivered in London in 1935, Lecture V concerns the psychology and treatment of transference. How this lecture arose is in itself a transference phenomenon, in that the audience wanted Jung to specifically talk about transference, which meant that he had to change his plans. Lecture V is his response to the audience's wishes.

The transference level, or the special language of the transference relationship, can be regarded as a kind of relational dream language. It can also be a special space that is always present—a kind of creative potential of the unconscious. However, how transference is articulated in the elliptical dialogue of analysis is not always obvious. Transference language has to be sensitively and carefully evaluated in relation to the level of a person's unconscious and the work in hand at this level. For example, when Björn came to the session with the image of the goddesses, it seemed clear to me that this archetypal projected transference image balanced the cold and awful experience with his father. This was not just personally projected material but was essentially archetypal and belonged to the collective unconscious archetypal field and to the self field. It also said something essential about what the analysand had invested in the relationship with the analyst. It had to do with the existential levels of life.

This is what Erich Neumann presents in his last lecture and published as the metapsychological essay *The Psyche and the Transformation of the Reality Planes* (Neumann 1960/1989.) This essay is a fruitful input to the containing ego-self attitude of the psychoanalyst. When we permit the ego-self axis to develop with the aid of the transcendent function, a view of reality as a unity of being is formed. When this is translated to analytical work, it can be understood as a rhythmic walking forward. On one side of the body, there is the differentiated, separatio, experienced reality, and on the other the nondual, coniunctio, experienced reality. In order to walk in any direction at all, both sides of the body and the mind are necessary. The self plane is where the ego is contained by the self and part of the self. In this plane, subject and object are united. The self *does* the seeing and hearing and does not concern itself with *what* is seen and heard. That is something that the more or less differentiated ego evaluates. Transference language is the undercurrent doing language and needs special attentiveness from the analyst. The language of the personal unconscious used in narratives, dreams, and images from childhood is significant for the analytical sessions. I refer to this as what ego language, because it is spoken and created from an ego that is both contained in and part of the self. The development of the analyst and analysand in their respective individuation processes, and the individuation of the analysis itself and what it relies and rests on, are based on a nonseparation from the self. The self is there and can be a curse but also a possibility, in that it has the potential to contribute telling archetypal images.

When Björn and I met again after the summer break, I decided to recognize and hold the transference image of the goddesses and not elaborate more on the image. After a break, the change and exchange in the analytical relationship is always a challenge for the two psychic worlds meeting and connecting. The map of the elliptical dialogue gives me an awareness of three dynamic powers of reciprocity, feedback, and resilience in the blue frame that need to be re-established.

Reciprocity refers to the two parties meeting again and unifying in the work in hand. Here, the focus is on the wish, longing, and meeting again, rather than being apart and separated. At the feedback level, the focus is on catching up with each other, and it is here that I received the goddess image as an archetypal message from Björn's self plane. With this feedback, he was prepared to work hard at making his father and mother complexes conscious, even though in his view the summer break had been too long. On the whole, I valued this, because we were resilient. We could connect and start working almost immediately with full psychic energetic flow. With hindsight, I may have been too optimistic in this evaluation and did not see his vulnerability in the regressed ego state Björn was in. However, when working with his childhood experiences, he came into contact with the ego states of hate and devaluation. This also meant that he had to take occasional breaks in the analytical process—which may also have been a way of punishing me for being in control of the process. At times, he would state that he was now thoroughly analysed and had no more work to do. He would also say that it was unfair that I did not reveal any of my own personal issues. For me, one of the first inner symbolic images from our first session continued, namely the image of a game of peekaboo and later one of hide-and-seek.

In her interesting article *Countertransference as Active Imagination: Imaginative Experiences of the Analyst*, published in the Journal of Analytical Psychology (JAP, 2007, 52, 413-431), Joy Schaverien discusses the imaginative experiences of the analyst. Here, her point is that the active imagination of the analyst as a countertransference activates the symbolic function in the analyst and thus contributes to the mediation of emergent consciousness in the analysand. Keeping the inner peekaboo image as a movement, I felt safe and confident that this was what Björn needed in order to build a more stable ego-self axis. My inner active imagination of the movement was also akin to keeping Wittgenstein's duck-rabbit image in constant aspect alternation. It held the tolerance of ambiguity and enabled me to empathize with Björn's (and my own) individuation process toward the emerging self. In our elliptical dialogue, the words and tempo slowed down when exploring childhood memories and how he later managed to continue his university studies, enter family life, and develop in his profession. In this process it came to a point where he was challenged to make a statement of commitment to the analytical work. Even though we had our usual appointment times, he sometimes did not turn up, although he could come to the following session. However, it reached a point where I felt the need to address the psyche's need for predictability, safety, and security. The peekaboo active imagination had reached a turning point and developed as it should for a child to feel secure in the relationship. The holding analyst/ mother was both present and consistent. The relationship was there, could take differentiation, and be a vessel for individuation. By this time, Björn's self-hatred had begun to decline to the extent that he could see himself as a cultivating gardener. However, in the actual transference with me, he went into a more erotic tension. Indeed, during the spring of our second year of analysis, our intimacy increased, with Björn having erotic fantasies about my body and drawing female bodies. He urged me to not be so prudish, wear loose clothing, and reveal more of my personal self. "You do not need to dress like a priest's wife. I want you to show more of your neckline!" I felt this to be intrusive and at times commented on the inappropriateness of his remarks. At other times, I just let it be. He had a kind of almost obsessive energy that also fueled his creativity. It may have been a mixture of all this that led to the *Father Murder* image and his wanting to embrace me. When I pulled back, he was furious, like a rejected boy/young man/lover all at the same time. As we had settled on the committed sessions, the only way to deal with this rupture was to work through it. However, at that particular moment, I was not even sure it that would be possible. This work became more of an exercise to keep the transcendent function going. For the following sessions, he arrived on time, and we spent them together with his now-furious energy that is described in the clinical Part II, when I had to listen to his monological language. Sometimes this became very repetitive, and at times I just wanted to say: "Oh, just stop it, let's get on with the essential work!" But for Björn this was essential transference work. It was also a question of tolerating the ambiguity and seeing that the individuation of the self that was necessary for the analytical treatment—again with reference to Wittgenstein to keep the alternation tolerance for the "duck-rabbit" or to Bateson to keep "a difference that makes a difference over time to be change." When in one session I asked him whether he could see any problems with wanting to hug, kiss, and be more personal with me, he did not understand the question. Björn felt no conscious sense of shame, perhaps because he was in a shamelessness that can be regarded as an extreme polarity of shame.

During my own sessions with my supervisor, this whole process was elaborated in terms of how to experience the transference between myself and Björn and at the parallel level between me and my supervisor. The ambiguity and tolerance for this was understood as that the goddess/erotic transference stood in the way of his individuation process, but at the same time was a presumption for it. I had also crossed professional boundaries that I was ashamed of. For example, I had visited the local art gallery with my husband when Björn had his art exhibition, and on my way to my practice through the park I had stopped and exchanged a few words with Björn, perhaps for too long. The boundary violations that became apparent to me during my own supervision made me conscious that Björn, with his infantile regressed attitude in combination with erotic transference and new creativity, was confused, and that was difficult for him to cope with. He was both surprised and furious and was caught up in a strong erotic transference that made him claim a full human relationship based on an outlived coniunctio experience. At an emotional symbolic level, I could understand this and also apply it to my own experience of crucial encounters with creative men. I began to realize how these relationships had influenced my own creativity and how easy it was to be both the seduced and the seducer, and thereby hinder creativity and the individuation process.

The crucial point here was whether Björn could work within the analytical frame and keep the personal intimate relationship there. He needed to make a statement about that, and I had to be firm. Jung's Lecture V on transference was also very helpful at this time and helped me to process transference into clinical understanding. At this point it is worth looking at the lecture a little more closely.

Jung begins his lecture on transference by defining the concept. First, at a general level it is defined as "an awkward hanging-on, an adhesive sort of relationship." In § 311 and the beginning of §312 CW 18 *The Tavistock Lectures*, Jung writes that "the term 'transference' is the translation of the German word *Übertragung*, which means to carry something over from one place to another. The word *Übertragung* is also used in a metaphorical sense to designate the carrying-over from one form to another. Therefore, in German it is synonymous with *Übersetzung*—that is, translation.

The psychological process of transference is a specific form of the more general process of projection. It is important to bring these two concepts together and to realize that transference is a special kind of projection—at least that is how I understand it. Of course, everybody is free to use the term in his own way."

In Björn's case, it means understanding projection and transference as unconscious mechanisms of an emotional and compulsory nature. As we have seen, Björn's emotions were sometimes overwhelming. Emotions are also contagious, as research and the discovery of the important mirror neurons have confirmed. Furthermore, as Jung says in his lecture: "It is even our duty as analysts to accept the emotions of the patient and to mirror them. That is the reason why I reject the idea of putting the patient on a sofa and sitting behind him. I put my patients in front of me and I talk to them as one natural human being to another, and I expose myself completely and react with no restriction" (CW 18, § 319).

As a consequence of this understanding of the intense transference relationship, it is important for the analyst to also be analysed and to have a father or mother confessor: "Even the Pope, for all his infallibility, has to confess regularly…If the analyst does not keep in touch with his unconscious objectively, there is no guarantee whatever that the patient will not fall into the unconscious of the analyst" (CW 18, § 323). This statement is a strong argument as to why all serious psychotherapists and psychoanalysts should have regular supervision and meet with peer groups to share inner thoughts and feelings about the analytical work. It creates an ethical space and is important for patient security and the analyst's ability to function well in a special healing relationship.

When discussing the etiology of transference, Jung is clear about the distinction to love. Transference only misuses love. However, it can be seen as a love at first sight, a passion beyond consciousness that can become an obsession about the analyst. This says a lot about the power that is involved, and, as an analyst, you have to be aware that as there is no common ground for the analysand to have such a relationship in the outer reality, the drive to build a relationship with the analyst is strong and characterised by passionate affect and erotic fantasy. This was relevant in Björn's case. He had found it difficult to form living, lasting relationships throughout his life. The gap and the feeling of inability to create contact were unconsciously overcome by building a bridge of compensation that was highly charged with erotic fantasies. But this has nothing to do with mature love, and the analyst needs to understand this in order to avoid being seduced in a covert, sublime, and, as sometimes happens, overt way. With this important background, the following four stages need to be made clear:

The first stage (§ 367 CW 18 *The Tavistock Lectures*) of working with transference is about establishing a mature attitude in the patient when seeing the world through the complexes and helping the analysand to see how the personal subjective images of his or her own father and mother are projected onto the analyst. This comes from a double perspective of seeing. One perspective is when we see the world through our personal experience of positive and negative authorities. The other perspective is having a mature attitude to the consciousness and subjective value of all the images that form our complexes. Concerning Björn, this is clearly shown in his images of his father, when he could talk about his similarity with his father and how this affected him, and also their differences. The subjective value was related to his reconnection to the God image. The father image was transformed into a higher value.

Jung talks about the process of the assimilation of the subjective value into the whole personality. In this first step, Jung means transference in terms of the relationship with the analyst and transference relationships with other important people in everyday life. The word "assimilation" is interesting. The process of assimilation is seen in relationship to the process of apperception, which means that a new content for the psyche is understood or apprehended in a passive or active way from both the ego perspective and the self perspective. It is a kind of soaking process of assimilation for the whole being. In Björn's case, the personal transference image of the punishing father was held in tension with the goddess transference image of me as his analyst. How these two images were allowed to do their work and how they were contained in our analytical hours in conjunction with a tolerance of ambiguity and image alternation is described in the dialogue below.

THE THERAPY OF THE TRANSFERENCE

In order to put transference into a category of its own in the fifth Tavistock Lecture, Jung talks about the therapy of the transference. What does this mean? Jung structures the therapy of the transference in four stages. In what follows, I name these stages one by one and illustrate them with images from the transference between Björn and myself, my comments on the analytical process, and thoughts about how I understand Jung's view of the transference.

The first stage: In practical terms, this means that the subjective value of the personal and impersonal content of the transference has to be realized by the analysand (CW 18, § 357). How is this manifested in the analytical relationship? In my work with Björn, this happened when we experienced a rupture and I confessed to having violated our boundaries. It was necessary to return to the blue frame and adjust that content to our analytical process. Coming and going without commitment for further work was destructive for our process. So the following dialogue developed:

Gunilla: It is crucial for our analysis if you can work within this analytical frame of our scheduled appointments. And Björn, you have to make a statement here.

Björn: Yes, yes, but it can be hard to come to the sessions when you are so important. It's as though I'm scared. I want to come so close in being intimate and at the same I'm scared. This makes me drop out.

Gunilla: Yes, I know that, and during the spring our intimacy increased, and I also crossed some professional boundaries. I should not have come to the art gallery with my husband. I should not have stopped to chat with you as long as I did in the park. These things confused you. Our analytical relationship belongs to the scheduled hours in my practice.

Björn: Yes, I see in one way, but yet... it's hard to understand; why can't you be more personal with me?

Gunilla: It's like an artist symbolizing strong emotions in images. You are an artist, and you have strong emotions. In your artistic work, your strong emotions are contained, and they emerge in symbolic form. Like the painting of the *Father Murder*. You have to shoot an arrow over the void in order to cope and perhaps make your father less threatening for you. Art for you is like a big container. While the feelings toward your father cannot be lived out concretely, at the symbolic level they can be made understandable and also change. It is the same with your inner image of me as a goddess. This is archetypal transference, and it has to stay at that level in our contained analytical frame. Only then can I help you to grow in this analytical container. But I do not want to put you behind a fence, so I will not now suggest a new appointment. When you have made your decision, you are welcome to set a time.

After a few days he sent me a text message to say that he had important things to tell me and wanted to make an appointment. In that session, my intention was to establish and renew the content of the blue frame within the elliptical dialogue, make the boundaries of our meeting clear and be open to what he brought with him.

From the perspective of analytical psychology and what this work brings into the elliptical dialogue, it is worth contemplating for a moment how the therapy of this transference can be understood. First, when working with archetypal projected figures, such as *The Little Goddesses with the Birds' Heads* and in the analytical process as a whole, it is easy to get inflated and confused by the strong energy that can emerge. In the illustration of the elliptical dialogue in depth dimension in Part I, this can be understood as the energy from both parties' self-fields. The differentiating separation movement is central here, in the sense that the analyst should communicate from the ego position without losing contact with the self and with his/her own archetypal plane and that of the analysand. For me, it was important to make a cognitive narrative of what the analytical work might look like. These feelings and expectations can be seen as natural, although acting on them in a boundary-crossing way as I did is not ethical. It is important to articulate that in order to avoid confusion and to acknowledge the strong energies in the analytical relationship.

When Björn's father complex began to discharge, so did the mother complex. Both complexes occupied his inner world less. The unconscious creative source was freed, and the complexes did not sap energy in the same way as before. The energy of the instincts became better balanced, and his creativity increased.

The second stage: Referring again to *Tavistock Lecture* number five: "Then we come to the *second stage* in the therapy of the transference. That is the *discrimination between personal and impersonal contents*" (CW 18, §368.) At first sight it can be hard to see the difference between stage one and two, but the importance is that when personal projections are dissolved by making them conscious, impersonal projections are not dissolved or banished because they belong to the structural elements of the psyche. They are not relics from the past to grow away from, but are important and valuable. Jung talks about dissolving the *act* of projection, but not dissolving its *contents*. The following intense session, in which Björn recounted "The Conference Dream," can be seen as an example of this.

THE CONFERENCE DREAM

When Björn and I meet again, he enters my practice saying, "You look beautiful!"

I say, "Thank you and welcome!"

"I've been working a lot, and if we lived together, you would see my living room. Drawings, colours, paper everywhere. You would have a nervous breakdown."

I say, "It seems to me you are in a very creative period."

"Yes and I've been thinking about our last session. I'm ambiguous when it comes to you. When I leave our sessions, I feel happy and fulfilled, but after a while, it turns to disappointment. It turns totally."

I say, "Do you have any idea what changes that?" (me, trying dialogical words.)

"No, but it is painful, and sometimes I think that it is this experience that makes me drop out of sessions and send you letters instead. It's the bipolar energy between desire for you and fear of you, and of coming to and going away from sessions that is so painful. But now that I'm here again, tell me what you think about this!"

I say, "Does it become more of a reality in the picture?"

"Don't rush me. I've told you my associations in front of the bathroom mirror: woman—unreachable, sexuality—unspeakable. You should have asked me more about that and not been so passive. I gave you hints of what was important. And more since we met in the park, I've been almost drunk by you, and I feel ashamed."

I say: "Let's slow down, and I'll share my ideas about your inner ambiguity and about coming and going and about me. Would you care to listen?"

I invite him to a dialogue, but first I have to see whether he can agree to listen. He sits in a more relaxed way, and I continue, slowly, and making myself conscious of my breathing at the same time, which is a way of calibrating myself to the ego-self axis and the transcendent function.

"Yes, yes, go on!"

I continue: "I know our relationship can be confusing and you feel frustrated about me. And I have done things that do not fit with an analytical work. I should not have come to the art gallery with my husband, and we should limit our appointments to this room. I should not have stopped and talked to you in the park. I think that these experiences with me outside my practice made you more confused and insecure and interfered with our work. I'm sorry about this. I should have been more conscious of it. My thoughts about this experience are that it may have made you furious and left you with mixed feelings of desire and longing at the same time. Combined with a strong energy and a desire for development and individuation, our work was partially blocked by the intense transference. This is my interpretation of what happened between us, and I wonder whether this might help you to understand the feeling of ambiguity about me and what makes you stop coming and then return?"

"Yes, yes, but now I want to tell you about the dream I had this morning!"

I continue: "First, we have to make a mutual agreement, and you have to make a clear statement to commit to our appointments so that can we be with each other here in my practice and work with inner images and with the creative art you make. Then we can see the symbolic meaning in growth and development. Do you think you can agree to keep our appointments here?"

"Yes, yes, and now I can perhaps see that this morning's dream might be of importance for the work to come. Can I continue?"

I say, "Let me listen to your dream."

"There's a conference. I attend, and Gunilla also attends; we might have arrived together. Now the conference is over, and I'm standing at the window on the upper floor. Then I see Gunilla leaving with another man, and I feel relieved. Relieved?! When I woke up, I was both confused and surprised. Why? Because if I was the one leaving with you, I would not have been able to leave you alone, we would have come into a conversation concerning our relationship and about building a home where we could live together. For me, this would have meant giving up my need for my own space. But I could not say that, because it would have meant that I was not a whole person and I would have been unveiled as an insecure person, and that had to be kept a secret. You see, I have not acknowledged my need for a space of my own. This was always a crucial point in my three marriages and led to divorce. My need to be alone to live separately at times is utterly important."

I say, "Yes it is utterly important for you to choose your own self, and I'm glad that you can acknowledge this basic need."

"But I choose this by crying inside. So this association to the woman is now false. I can and must choose myself. I have seen this unbalance earlier as depression. Yes, that's the result." He leans back in the chair, relaxed and calm, and says: "It's about time that I become aware and can make this choice. Now I understand why I'm so relieved about seeing you leaving the conference with someone else. I am in myself and conscious of this in my dream."

I say, "It's dangerous to deny parts of yourself, but now you have taken them on board."

"Yes, and now I would like to kiss your knee! And I think that you should give your admirer a reward, a twinkle or so. That would enrich you as a woman I'm sure!"

I'm thinking that the erotic attraction has been a motor here and also that it did not made me lose patience. I remember smiling in the moment.

He then asks, "Do we see each other again?"

I say, "Do you want to schedule another appointment?"

"No, I don't need that now."

I say, "Then when you call, we can continue and set up another appointment."

"Or you call."

I say: "No, I will not call you, that's not a part of our analytical agreement. It is important to respect your integrity and own space. When you feel ready for another appointment, you should know that I am here for you, and we can work together."

"I don't think I need that now."

We say goodbye.

When Jung talks about the second stage of the therapy of the transference, it refers to the discrimination between personal and impersonal contents. The crucial analytical process here is to dissolve the act of projection, not its contents. The conference dream, together with the image of the birds' head goddesses and his wanting to kiss my knee, forms a numinous energetic field. Jung borrows the concept of the numinous from the German theologian Rudolf Otto (1869-1937) and how it is described his book *Das Heilige—The Idea of the Holy* (1917.) Jung introduces this concept into analytical psychology and widens the concept to enhance experiences of strong religious and spiritual quality to what in analytical psychology can be identified as a symbolic expression of the self-field, following both Jung and Neumann. This is similar to the development of the ego-self axis in the second half of life, where the self-field moves toward the archetypal field and where the inner and outer reality planes develop into one reality field (Neumann 1952). This should not be mixed up with a blurred reality, where the archetypal field merges with the ego function and takes over the whole psychic experience, which can lead to the development of psychotic states.

Gregory Bateson talks about being aware of 'patterns that connect' and that these patterns can be experienced as the unification of mind and matter. In the map of the elliptical dialogue, where analytical psychology and systems theory connect with language theory in the relational holding of multiple layers of the psyche in movement and creativity. These are the ground energies of the self planes that we try to make visible and conscious in analytical work. This is relational seeing and seeing into the white spaces of the elliptical dialogue, where Hermes' liminal experience leads to consciousness that can be brought into language and dialogue.

In this second stage, Björn's psyche dissolved this hard transference in his inner world by seeing the continuation of the dream with me walking away with another man and making him conscious about his need to have his own space and be alone.

What happened next in our work? We met again, and this time our work developed into a regular two sessions a week. As a background to the new entry, Björn sent a letter beginning with the word "Why?" Here he refers to the rupture and a feeling of being baffled. He was also clear that he was the one stepping out of my office, but yet "why and why was I both attacked by and attached to the Rottweiler?" He continued, "Yes, I fell in love with you—with the image I had created of you. But not in you. I'm not prone to falling in love in a person I do not know. But the image of you was confusing for me, and I can now see a bit of why I felt so rejected when you did not embrace me when entering with the Father Murder image. Maybe I was too small and mixed up with feelings of passion and a need to be received like a little boy; this was too much for me."

With this letter, and the work that followed, the analytical process made a breakthrough in that the intense transference did not stand in the way for the individuation process. Björn worked on important issues. He had passed the first stage of romantic love where you want to be everything for your partner and your partner wants to fulfill everything for you. In the long run, this is an unacceptable stage, and you have to negotiate how to separate. From "I want all of you" to more ego life.

In the map of the elliptical dialogue, the unconscious tensions have been made more conscious with the aid of images, dreams, and actions. As these have now been articulated, the differentiating and separating movement is more in focus. With the language, dialogue, and life that was emerging, Björn and I were able to proceed.

In my own supervision, I could see that my analytical attitude was sometimes too passive and at other times too defensive, even seductive in a subtle way. It was important to interpret Björn's wish to kiss my knee as an expression of gratitude and to see the erotic aspect of this in a metaphorical way. At times there had been too much fire under the alchemical pot. For me, when Björn was physically demonstrative, I pulled back and became defensive. He—his Pan instinct—was too overwhelming. This was very difficult to meet in a balanced way, because at the same time as he was overstimulated. I also had to signal he was very special and affirm him in that way.

In the Freudian tradition, we might have interpreted this specific transference action from the disillusional perspective as resistance and then analyzed the disillusional quality of the action. In the Jungian psychoanalytical way, we try to carry the transference and interpret it symbolically. From this standpoint, it is important to take care of the transcendent function necessary for the ego-self axis to develop. This balancing and moderating of the fire is important in order to avoid fanning one side of it. I now think that the ruptures in our dialogue stemmed from these difficulties. I am not saying that ruptures should be avoided in the analytical work. That is impossible. My argument is that when they occur, they can be seen relationally and symbolically and, in this way, enrich the individuation journey for both the analysand and the analyst. However, it is the responsibility of the analyst to be aware of them consciously and ethically, and that the analyst benefits from this in his/her professional and personal individuation process. This part of our work can serve as an illustration of the third stage of the therapy of the transference.

The third stage: In lecture five, Jung says: "On the account of this tremendous dynamic power of archetypal images you cannot reason them away. Therefore the only thing to do at the third stage of the therapy of the transference is to *differentiate the personal relationship to the analyst from impersonal factors*. It is perfectly understandable that when you have carefully and honestly worked for a patient, he likes you, and because you have done a decent bit of work on a patient, you like him, whether it is a man or a woman. … A personal human reaction to you is normal and reasonable, therefore let it be, it deserves to live; it is not transference any more. But such an attitude to the analyst is possible in him and decent form only when it is not vitiated by unrecognized impersonal values. This means that it has to be, on the other side, a full recognition of the importance of the archetypal images, many of which have a religious character" (CW 18 *The Tavistock Lectures*, Lecture V § 373).

Toward the end of this part of our work, when there was a calmer atmosphere between us, Björn presented me with the *Facing the Void* transference image. The image portrays a seated couple, connected at the tail but with space between them, surrounded by nature in the form of birds, the moon, flowers, and trees. It is a safe place for seeing into the openness of what is to come and what has passed. This image was also connected to the following text: "We sit inside a deep forest. The forest is in darkness, yes, it is so dark that you can hardly see the path. This is dangerous but not life-threatening, if you are able to have a direction and a goal. If you have a goal and know where you are aiming, you are able to discover the path that leads out of the wood."

Facing the Void - Photo reprinted with permission from Björn

The analytical relationship had by now become more differentiated and stable in a working alliance that served the growth of Björn's individuation process. As we were no longer stuck and mixed with the archetypal field, the energy was more flexible. Archetypes no longer threatened to overwhelm the ego and cause confusion, and boundaries no longer needed to be tested. We had regular sessions in which we were able to work at the symbolic level, where Björn's self and ego were developing. From my perspective, my maternal empathy had changed toward the more paternal side of me, where I could be freer in my own energy. The image also suggested that there was a deep ontological connection with our living ecological surroundings. The ego-self axis comes to life in the image represented by the trees growing from earth to heaven and inhabited by the surveying bird. The living ego-self position is also clear about the importance of having life goals. The ego-self axis then developed at both the intrapsychic and interpersonal levels, which resonated with the second stage of development in Neumann's structure of the growth of the ego-self axis in the second half of life (Neumann 1952).

The fourth stage: Again referring to Jung's fifth lecture: "I call this fourth stage the therapy of the transference the *objectivation of impersonal images*. It is an essential part of the process of individuation. Its goal is to detach consciousness from the object so that the individual no longer places the guarantee of his happiness, or his life even, in factors outside himself, whether they be persons, idea, or circumstances, but comes to realize that everything depends on whether he holds the treasure or not. If the possession of that gold is realized, then the centre of gravity is in the individual and no longer in an object on which he depends" (CW 18 The *Tavistock Lectures*, Lecture V § 377).

The spiritual dimension is central in Jung's view of the human psyche and is also present in the works of Gregory Bateson and Ludwig Wittgenstein. In this respect, they share a common ground. In this fourth stage, Jung talks about the treasure and how in religious traditions this is projected into sacred figures and historical symbols that are no longer so relevant today. This forces the individual to find the own unique way of expressing the spiritual dimension in his or her life. In analytical psychology, exploring this way can be made with the help of active imagination. That was what Jung wanted to tell the audience about in his fifth Tavistock Lecture. But as indicated earlier, transference comes to the fore in strong analytical work and also in a strong dialogue with an audience when lecturing. It is therefore necessary to consciously deal with transference and have a structure for this. However, the fourth stage not just can be seen as developing active imagination as the spiritual function in analysis but also as active imagination from the perspective of the analyst in the analytical process. In the work with Björn, an example of this is my strong inner image of a peekaboo game that developed into hide-and-seek. This can be understood as a movement toward setting boundaries and defining the blue frame in the different stages of our work. By holding and letting the image unfold within myself, this countertransference became clear. In my understanding of this fourth stage and how it corresponds to the map of the elliptical dialogue, I expand the understanding and practice of active imagination to include the

The Flying Rug - Photo reprinted with permission from Björn

analyst in the specific analytical journey. The images that grew inside me stemmed from how I perceived our relationship. It became a Mobius strip movement, where the various images, reflections, and positions changed and eventually led me to make more conscious choices and interventions in our work, such as addressing a more mature ego position and demanding a statement of commitment to the regular frame of the analysis. This can also be seen as me changing from a maternal position in our relationship to a paternal one and demanding a more stable ego-self axis from Björn.

Contemporary Jungian analysts have written about this particular perspective of active imagination in the analyst during analytical work. I have earlier referred to Joy Schaverien (2007) but both Jan Wiener in *The Therapeutic Relationship* (2009) and Murray Stein in *Soul: Treatment and Recovery* (2016) refers to the inner potential of finding meaning in life through careful work in the analytical relationship. Staying alert and awake in your own countertransference images is a bit like twisting and turning the red circle strip or turning toward the consciousness of the black ego point and "reading" it with your inner instruments of feeling, thinking, sensing, and intuition. The reading can then become a dynamic tool in the active imagination process. It also enables you to interpret images in a hermeneutical spiral movement that at the same time has the dynamic movement of a Mobius strip. Language and images are closely related internally and externally in the green elliptical line of the map.

In this fourth stage, I think that Jung is pointing to the fact that neurotic symptoms can also be an expression of unsatisfied spiritual needs and that by incorporating them into the therapy of the transference, he gives room for the spiritual symbols to grow in each individual. This is done by linking the symbols in a chain of higher numinous images and symbols of the self and giving them enough space for the discovery and recovery of the spiritual realm. His basic assumption is that the religious function works in the human unconscious like a rhizome—an underground tuber that contains roots and shoots.

The illustration of the flying rug that Björn presented me with toward the end of our work can be seen as the threads of the many neurotic complexes that now took the form of a rug. A home-woven rug consists of strips cut from old clothes, sheets, towels, and other textiles used in the home and recycled into something new and useful.

Björn explained that he could now let go of the old memories and pain because they had been transformed into something new. At the same time, clean white sheets hung in the air like promises for a future life.

The development of Björn's belief system in this phase of our analytical work was interesting. He had been involved in different Christian congregations but had struggled with the Fifth Commandment to honour your father and mother and how this could now be assimilated in a new way in his psyche. As he became freed from his complexes, he gained more access to the transcendent function and its energy flow in the ego-self axis, which led to changes in his spiritual relationship. It moved from seeing God as a subject and as personified toward recognizing a spiritual power that could energize all the dimensions of his life. This emerged in some of our dialogues as important dreams and his decision about where he wanted to be buried when that time came. He wanted to be rooted in his childhood landscape. It was as though the mystical parts of life were allowed to remain in their mystical creative states and did not necessarily have to be analyzed. In this respect, the spoken word has its limitations and has to be formulated as metaphors. Religious belief systems also develop in the maturing individuation process. In Björn's case, he became more attuned to Bible passages, such as Luke 17:21, "The Kingdom of God is within you."

He explained: "This is deeply true now for me, and as I read Chassidism with a text that says something like God does not expect you to be like Moses but expects you to become more of yourself as a whole person. Then I can let go of the right or wrong way of believing in God. I can just go on and try to live as fully as I can."

Toward the end of our work we had several enlightening sessions that were characterized by calm and presence. These were I-thou meetings at a deep level, both in words and beyond words, filled with mutual respect and love.

PART III
THREE THEORIES IN
THE ELLIPTICAL DIALOGUE –
THE SYNTHESISING,
INTEGRATIVE PART

12. The elliptical dialogue as a communication model for psychotherapy

Throughout this book, I have wandered in the borderland of three concepts: the map of the elliptical dialogue; the three theories (systems theory, language theory and the theory of analytical psychology); and the concept of clinical experience. Here, the analytical work with Björn is a visible process that illustrates the integration of practice and theory into the map of the elliptical dialogue (described by different dimensional illustrations).

This is also a book about integrating theories into a new map of orientation for the psychological, spiritual, and dialogical relationship that is present in psychotherapy, psychoanalysis, and supervision. The need to create this map came from a desire to understand and orient in analytical practice. In this sense, I think that we all create maps of understanding inside and outside ourselves, whether we are aware of it or not.

In the first part of this book, two images from Vermeer are included called "the geographer" and "the astronomer." Returning to those images and reflecting on the meaning of making maps, you could say that making maps of order in times of chaos and stress is archetypal. A map weaves together a picture and a narrative and can be a powerful statement that reveals where I am and where I want to go. The map then has a dual purpose and can also be a noun or a verb. "A map" and "to map" reflect a subject and a movement. The elliptical dialogue aims to work in this way and be a useful tool in the psychotherapeutic practice.

In both theory and practice, there is always development, whether we like it or not. The making of hypothesis in clinical work, the mapping of our own inner experiences as we make ourselves present in the clinical and supervisory experience and the reflective consideration of what kind of system we are part of and how this is connected to wider patterns is up to our ego function to be put into words—or not. It is up to us to assess the development of our own ego-self function and, as psychotherapists, psychoanalysts, and supervisors, there is the ethical responsibility of being in tune with our own ego-self axis. Asking questions is useful, such as: Is the work at hand useful and creative? Does it support a movement that I can refer to playfully? Does it have an integrative connection of helpful theory and practice?

Common to all the three thinkers in the elliptical dialogue is the creation of a playful and creative attitude of mind that is connected to nature. Wittgenstein had to withdraw to the dramatic nature in Skjolden, Norway, to contain his powerful energy and transform it into words as *Tractatus logico-philosophicus* (1921, 1922, 1961, 1992) that them became the basis of his language theory. Bateson placed himself among animals and plants in nature in order to develop systems theory as described in *Mind and Nature* (1979, 1987). Jung started by playing with stones and connecting to nature in that way, which led to his poetic writings in *Septem Sermones ad Mortuos* (2009) and his map of the mind and soul in *Systema Munditotius* (2009), together with the more structured outline of the theory of analytical psychology in Psychological Types (1921, 1981).

The fundamental movements of the mind, the self field of nature, mapping, and the spiritual connection are common to all human beings and are present as rhizomes, ready to make themselves visible in our own lives.

I would like to end the book with a fairy tale and a reconnection to the underlying energetic source symbolized by the trickster god Hermes.

THE ELLIPTICAL DIALOGUE SEEN IN A FAIRY TALE OF TRANSFORMATION—ESPEN ASHTWADDLER

Some years ago, when it was suggested that I might write a book about the elliptical dialogue, my immediate reaction was: "No, you are not able to do that!" but also "You never know…" The passion was already there, and when locating myself somewhere between these inner voices, an old Norwegian fairy tale came to mind. Here, then, is the fairy tale about Espen Ashtwaddler. As with every relationally told story, the language arranges itself differently and changes with every teller:

It is about a king and his daughter, the princess, of whom he was very fond and proud due to her beauty and wisdom. What he liked most was her laughter, which was impossible to define but full of pleasure. One day she was no longer able to laugh. In his desperation, the king declared that the man who was able to make her laugh again would be given a reward. The reward could be small or large, but as yet was unknown. But those who tried but failed to make her laugh would have their backs sliced and salted.

Many young men came to the castle to try their luck. Among them were three brothers: Per, Pål, and Espen Askeladd. The two first names are somewhat international, Per (Peter) and Pål (Paul), but Espen is purely Norweigan. The second name Askeladd, translates into English as Ash-twaddler. Espen Ashtwaddler. He got this name because he liked to spend his days by the fire, playing with the ashes and thinking. His brothers mocked him constantly for that.

When the two brothers Per and Pål took off for the castle, they had trained themselves well — Per by reading a big book of laws and Pål by reading another big book that taught him all the Latin words.

They were stunned to see Espen following behind them. "Go home!" they screamed, "You will never make it!" Espen, ignoring his brothers' warnings, looked around curiously as he always did. As his eyes fell on a crow's wing, he cried out to his brothers, "I found, I found, I found a crow's wing."

"Throw it away," they said.

"No. You never know what it might be used for!" he answered and put it in his pocket.

Not long after he cried out again, "I found, I found an old shoe!"

"Throw it away, it's good for nothing," they said.

But Espen put it in his pocket, saying, "You never know."

The third time he cried: "I found, I found a piece of red clay!"

"Ugh, throw it away," they replied again, but Espen put the clay in his pocket saying, "You never know."

Per was the first to enter the castle to meet the princess. He said, "It is hot in here."

"It is hotter in the oven," she replied.

Per, confused, couldn't speak and had his back inevitably sliced and salted. Pål was similarly confused and, as he stumbled to find the right words, he was also taken away, sliced and salted.

When Espen entered and said the same thing, and the princess replied as before, Espen replied, "Good, then I can have my crow's wing cooked." "What will you use for cooking?" she asked. Pulling the piece of clay out of his pocket, he said, "I will just wrap this around the wing!" "But the broth will leak out," she said. "No," Espen said, "I will collect the broth in this," and pointed to the old shoe.

The princess, dumbfounded, started to laugh, as did the king and his servants. So as promised, Espen Ashtwaddler had his reward.

This fairy tale can be understood in many ways, but it protects movement and creativity of the self between a definite "No" and "You never know".

The crow's wing, the red clay, and the old shoe all serve as transformers for Espen, but had no meaning in themselves without the connecting dialogue between himself and the princess. Espen collected the items he found and put them in his pocket for future use. If we play around a little with the symbols in the fairy tale, it could be said that Gregory Bateson, with his mind and nature, is symbolized by the crow's wing. Ludwig Wittgenstein could be seen as the piece of clay, as changeable as our relational language. Espen's journey, and putting the objects—the crow's wing, the piece of clay, and the shoe—in his pocket, can serve as a symbol for the elliptical dialogue grounded in the analytical psychology of C. G. Jung.

HERMES AS TRANSFORMER IN THE ELLIPTICAL DIALOGUES

The Greek god Hermes has been an energetic symbol throughout this book. However, in the three theories of the elliptical dialogue, his appearance has changed. In systems theory as explained by Gregory Bateson, Hermes was portrayed in the concept of cybernetics. Seeing, being, and talking relationally into patterns that connect reflect an epistemology that is based on caring for the ecology of mind. Hermes can also be seen at work in the "duck-rabbit" image that Wittgenstein used for alternations. From this, conclusions can be drawn about how to use language in the analytical setting, where the participant's ability to be in language in an interplay with others focuses on new narratives of the self for individuation and creativity. Seeing and using language from the perspective of change and exchange will make the participants sensitive to what is in-formation and ex-formation in the elliptical dialogue, where the grammar of sight is apparent in the words and the language. As in Vermeer's paintings of the two women—one with two hearts beating in her and the other holding weighing scales—this can be seen as a hermeneutic image for a language based on reciprocity, feedback, and resilience in order to keep and preserve movement in integrity.

In analytical psychology and its clinical applications, Hermes is often thought of as an appearance in the context of synchronicity and meaning making. For Jung, synchronicity was the emergence of a meaningful coincidence. The classical Jungian psychoanalytical example of this is Jung in a session with a young woman who was struggling in a very intellectual way with herself and her understanding of herself. One day she recounted a dream in which she had been given a golden scarab. What happened next was that there was a tap on the window behind where Jung was sitting. Both of them heard this, Jung turned around and "opened the window and caught the creature in the air as it flew in. It was the nearest analogy to a golden scarab that one finds in our latitudes, a scarabaeidae beetle, the common rose-shafer (*Cetonia aurata*), which contrary to its usual habits, had evidently felt an urge to get into a dark room at this particular moment" (CW 8, § 843 *Synchronicity: an acausal connecting principle* 1952). In synchronicity there is an inner psychic event, in this case the woman's dream in which she was given a golden scarab, and an outer physical event, here the scarabaeidae beetle tapping on the window. Both emerged in the session and created astonishment and amazement. But a third factor is also necessary, which is about Jung opening the window and making meaning of the event by putting this experience into words so that the woman's individuation process could develop further. These three factors together form the synchronistic experience. This simultaneous coincidence is something that we can be open to in our own everyday life experiences and be transformed by. This can be seen as Hermes' energetic appearance in the elliptical dialogue. His energy blows in, open windows, and crosses borders in unexpected ways. His energy crosses over and engages participants to unfold and work on meaning and development.

In Jung's last essay (CW 18, § 590 *Symbols and the interpretations of dreams*) composed shortly before his death in June 1961, there is passage in the text Healing the Split that gives clear direction to the use of language and words in dialogue and relationship. Language, words, and symbols that are charged with numinosity, or psychic energy, are dynamic and will have consequences. They acquire life and meaning when we try to learn about their numinosity and their relationship to the individual. The way in which they are related to you and me, to us, is all-important. In following the symbols in dreams and inner imaginations and their content in the language of nature, the relational seeing in language sets us the task of translating these concepts into contemporary dialogues with words that are connected to our spirit of the depths and to the spirit of our time.

The three thinkers presented in this book were aware of the content in the language of nature and in the enormous responsibility that lies in the task of not dehumanizing language but connecting it to relationship for ongoing dialogues. The map of the elliptical dialogue as presented here can hopefully serve as a portable three-dimensional symbol for individuation journeying that includes curiosity about personal and professional life.

REFERENCES

Auerswald, E.W. (1987) Epistemological Confusion in Family Therapy and Research. In *Family Process* 26: 317 – 330.

Aron L. (1996, 2001, 2009) *A Meeting of Minds.* New York, London: Routledge.

Bachelard, G. (1960/1969) *The Poetics of Reverie.* Boston: Beacon Press.

Bachtin, M. (1920/1997) *Det dialogiska ordet.* Gråbo: Anthropos.

Bateson, G. (1972), *Steps to an ecology of mind.* St Albans and New York.

Bateson, G. (1979/2002) *Mind and Nature. A Necessary Unity.* Cresskill, NJ: Hampton Press.

Bateson, G. and Bateson M.C. (1987/2005) *Angels Fear. Towards an Epistemology of the Sacred.* Cresskill, NJ: Hampton Press.

Bateson, N. (2011) *A Daughters's Portrait of Gregory Bateson. An Ecology of Mind. Remember the Future.* A film by Nora Bateson, Mindjazz pictures.

Bauer, J. (2007) *Varför jag känner som du känner. Intuitiv kommunikation och hemligheten med spegelneuronerna.* Stockholm: Natur och Kultur German title: *Warum ich füle, was du fülst – Intuitive Kommunikation und das Geheimnis der Speigelneurone.* (2005) Hamburg: Hoffman und Kampe Verlag.

Berg, L. (2005) *Gryning över Kalahari, hur människan blev människa.* Stockholm: Ordfront. English title: *Dawn over Kalahari: how humans became humans.* (2005/2011.)

Bibel 2000 Göteborg: Cordia.

Brand, S. ed. (1974, 1980) *The Next Whole Earth Catalogue.* San Francisco: Point Foundation (distribution Penguin),1.

Brown, A. (1988) Language and the emerging symbol. In *Journal of Analytical Psychology*, 1988, Vol 33, Issue 3, p 277-297.

Buschor, E. (1940) *Griechische Vasen. Mit 282 Abbildungen.* München: Verlag R. Piper & Co.

Cambray, J. and Carter, L. (2004) *Analytical Psychology. Contemporary Perspectives in Jungian Analysis.* Hove and New York: Brunner-Routledge.

Cambray, J. (2009/2012) *Synchronicity. Nature & Psyche in an Interconnectd Universe.* Texas: Texas A&M University Press College Station.

Charlton, N. G. (2008) *Understanding Gregory Bateson, Mind, Beauty and the Sacred Earth.* Albany: the State University of New York Press.

Cixous, H. (1975/2015) *Medusas Skratt.* Stockholm: Modernista. French title: *Le Rire de la Méduse.*

Colman, W. (2005) Sexual metaphor and the language of unconscious phantasy. In *Journal of Analytical Psychology*, 2005, Vol 50, Issue 5, p 641-660.

Connolly, A. (2002) To speak in tongues: language, diversity and psychoanalysis. In *Journal of Analytical Psychology*, 2002, Vol 47, Issue 3, p 359-382.

Evetts-Secker, J. (2012) *At Home in the Language of the Soul.* New Orleans, Louisiana: Spring Journal Books.

Fairbairn, W.R.D. (1952/1999) *Psychoanalytic Studies of the Personality.* London and New York: Routledge,

Fosha, D. ed. (2009) *The Healing Power of Emotion. Affective Neuroscience, Development & Clinical Practice.* New York, N.Y.: W.W. Norton & Company Ltd.

Fredriksson, G. (1993) *Wittgenstein.* Stockholm: Albert Bonniers förlag.

Gadamer, H-G. (2003) *Den gåtfulla hälsan.* Ludvika: Dualis. German title: *Über die Verborgenheit der Gesundheit.*

Jastrow, J. (1900) *Fact and Fable in Psychology.* Boston: Houghton Mifflin.

Jung. C.G. (1907/1981) *The Psychology of Dementia Praecox.* In *Collected Works* 3. London: Routledge & Kegan Paul.

Jung, C.G. (1916/1958, 1959./1981) *The Transcendent Function.* In *Collected Works* 8. London: Routledge & Kegan Paul.

Jung, C.G. (1921/1981) *Definitions.* In *Collected Works* 6, London: Routledge & Kegan Paul.

Jung, C.G. (1933/1934./1981) *A Study in the Process of Individuation.* In *Collected Works* 9i. London: Routledge & Kegan Paul.

Jung, C.G. (1946/1981) *The Psychology of the Transference.* In *Collected Works* 16. London: Routledge & Kegan Paul.

Jung, C.G. (1935/1977) *The Tavistock Lectures.* In *Collected Works* 18. London: Routledge & Kegan Paul.

Jung, C.G. (1937/1981) *Psychological Factors Determining Human Behaviour.* In *Collected Works* 8. London: Routledge & Kegan Paul.

Jung, C.G. (1938/1981) *Modern Psychology Offers a Possibility of Understanding.* In *Collected Works* 13. London: Routledge & Kegan Paul.

Jung, C.G., with Aniela Jaffé (1961/1989) *Memories, Dreams, Reflections.* New York: Random House.

Jung, C.G. (1961/1977) *Healing the Split.* In *Collected Works* 18. London: Routledge & Kegan Paul.

Jung, C.G. (2009) *The Red Book.* Ed. Sonu Shamdasani. New York: W.W. Norton & Co.

Kerényi, Karl. (1976/2003.) *Hermes, Guide of Souls.* Putnam, CT.: Spring Publications, Inc.

Kohut, H. (1971.) *The Analysis of the Self.* New York: International Universities Press.

Lech, B. (2012.) *Consciousness about own and others' affects.* Linköping University.

Luepnitz (1988.) Batesons heritage: Bitter fruit. In *Family Therapy Networker,* sept/okt 1988.

Maturana, H. Varela F. (1987) *The Tree of Knowledge.* Boston: New Science Library.

Monk, R. (1990/1992) *Ludwig Wittgenstein – Geniets Plikt.* Göteborg: Daidalos. English title: *Ludwig Wittgenstein - The Duty of Genius.* Jonathan Cape Ltd.

Nationalencyklopedin (1993) *Nationalencyklopedin, Band 10.* Höganäs: Bra Böcker AB.

Neumann, E. (1952/1973) *Amor and Psyche, The Psychic Development of the Feminine, A Commentary on the Tale by Apuleius.* New York: Princeton/Bollingen Paperback Edition, Third Printing.

Neumann, E. (1973/1990) *The Child.* Boston: Shambhala.

Neumann, E. (1952/1989) *The Psyche and the Transformation of the Reality Planes: A Metapsychological Essay.* In The Place of Creation. Princeton, NJ: Princeton University Press.

Paperback Oxford English Dictionary. (1979/2012) Oxford: University Press

Rilke, R.M. (1967/1998) *Duinoelegierna.* Stockholm: Bonnier.

Schaverein, J. (2007) Countertransference as active imagination: imaginative experiences of the analyst. In *The Journal of Analytical Psychology* (JAP, 2007, 52, 413-431.)

Shotter, J. (2008) *Conversational Realities Revisited: Life, Language, Body and World.* Chagrin Falls, Ohio: Taos Institute Publications.

Stern, D. (2004) *The Present Moment in Psychotherapy and Everyday Life.* New York: W.W. Norton.

Stein, M. ed. (2010) *Jungian Psychoanalysis. Working in the Spirit of C.G. Jung.* Chicago and La Salle, Illinois: Open Court.

Stein, M. (2014) *Minding the Self. Jungian Meditations on Contemporary Spirituality.* London and New York: Routledge.

Stein, M. (2016) *Soul: Treatment and Recovery. The selected works of Murray Stein.* London and New York: Routledge.

Tomkins, S.S. (1962) *Affect, Imagery, Consciousness, Vol I: The Positive Affects.* New York: Springer.

Tomkins, S.S. (1963) *Affect, Imagery, Consciousness, Vol II: The negative affects.* New York: Springer.

Tranströmer, T. (1997/2011) *New Collected Poems.* Northumberland: Bloodaxe Books.

Tronick, E. (2007) https://www.youtube.com/watch?v=bg89qxw30bm

Vatne, H. (1991) *Ludwig Wittgenstein i Skjolden* Booklet published by Luster Kommune.

Watzlawick P., Beavin Bavelas J., Jackson D. D. (1967) *Pragmatics of human communication. A study of interactional patterns, pathologies and paradoxes.* New York, London: W.W. Norton & Company.

Wiener, J. (2009) *The Therapeutic Relationship.* Texas: Texas A&M University Press College Station.

Wiener, N. (1948) *Cybernetics: Or Control and Communication in the Animal and in the Machine.* Cambridge: M.I.T. Press.

Wittgenstein, L. (1921/2005): *Tractatus logico-philosophicus.* Stockholm: Thales. German title: *Logisch-philosophische Abhandlung.*

Wittgenstein, L. (1921/1961): *Tractatus Logico-Philosophicus.* London: Routledge & Kegan Paul

Wittgenstein L. (1953/1996): *Filosofiska undersökningar.* Stockholm: Thales. German and English title: *Philosophische Untersuchungen/ Philosophical Investigations.*

von Bertalanffy, L. (1968/1973) *General Systems Theory.* London: Penguin Books.

Gunilla Midbøe, MSW., certified psychotherapist, supervisor and Jungian psychoanalyst, works in private practice in the western parts of Sweden. She is a board member of the Jungian Foundation in Sweden, editor for the net journal Coniunctio and a board member of the Danish Society of Analytical Psychology, as well as a member of DSAP's training committee. She has presented clinical papers at IAAP conferences in Vilnius, St Petersburg and congress in Kyoto, written articles and lectures within the field of analytical psychology. Her main spheres of interest include how symbols and language interact and contribute to individuation within the analytical relationship and the development of contemporary analytical psychology.

Visit her website at
www.gunillaMidbøe.se.

www.ingramcontent.com/pod-product-compliance
Lightning Source LLC
Chambersburg PA
CBHW040140270326
41928CB00022B/3279